ClearRevise®

AQA GCSE
French 8652

Illustrated revision and practice

Foundation and Higher

Marie-Thérèse Bougard

Published by
PG Online Limited
The Old Coach House
35 Main Road
Tolpuddle
Dorset
DT2 7EW
United Kingdom

sales@pgonline.co.uk
www.clearrevise.com
www.pgonline.co.uk
2024

PREFACE

Absolute clarity! That's the aim.

This is everything you need to ace your exams and beam with pride. Each topic is laid out in a beautifully illustrated format that is clear, approachable and as concise and simple as possible.

We have included worked examination-style questions with answers for each of the four papers. This helps you to understand where marks are coming from and to familiarise yourself with the style of questions you will be asked. There is also a set of exam-style questions at the end of each section for you to practise your responses. You can check your answers against those given at the end of the book.

A full **transcript** and **audio clips** can be downloaded from the **clearrevise.com** website, along with tips on how to approach the listening paper and guidance on marking each of the questions.

ACKNOWLEDGEMENTS

Every effort has been made to trace and acknowledge ownership of copyright. The publisher will be happy to make any future amendments with copyright owners where it has not been possible to make contact. The publisher would like to thank the following companies and individuals who granted permission for the use of their images or material in this textbook.

Design and artwork: Jessica Webb / PG Online Ltd

All Sections
Photographic images: © Shutterstock
Street musicians © esperanza casso / Shutterstock.com, Battle of the Flowers © DARRAY / Shutterstock.com,
Festival Canarias © criben / Shutterstock.com, Annecy © Rostislav Glinsky / Shutterstock.com,
Rubbish bins © FreeProd33 / Shutterstock.com, Arcachon tourists © JeanLucIchard / Shutterstock.com

First edition 2024 10 9 8 7 6 5 4 3 2 1
A catalogue entry for this book is available from the British Library
ISBN: 978-1-916518-00-1
Author: Marie-Thérèse Bougard
Editor: Jenny Gwynne
Copyright © PG Online 2024
All rights reserved
No part of this publication may be reproduced, stored in a retrieval system, or transmitted in any form or by any means without the prior written permission of the copyright owner.

This product is made of material from well-managed FSC®-certified forests and from recycled materials.

Printed by Bell and Bain Ltd, Glasgow, UK.

THE SCIENCE OF REVISION

Illustrations and words

Research has shown that revising with words and pictures doubles the quality of responses by students.[1] This is known as 'dual-coding' because it provides two ways of fetching the information from our brain. The improvement in responses is particularly apparent in students when they are asked to apply their knowledge to different problems. Recall, application and judgement are all specifically and carefully assessed in public examination questions.

Retrieval of information

Retrieval practice encourages students to come up with answers to questions.[2] The closer the question is to one you might see in a real examination, the better. Also, the closer the environment in which a student revises is to the 'examination environment', the better. Students who had a forthcoming test 2–7 days away did 30% better using retrieval practice than students who simply read, or repeatedly reread material. Students who were expected to teach the content to someone else after their revision period did better still.[3] What was most interesting in other studies is that students using retrieval methods and testing for revision were also more resilient to the introduction of stress.[4]

Ebbinghaus' forgetting curve and spaced learning

Ebbinghaus' 140-year-old study examined the rate at which we forget things over time. The findings still hold true. However, the act of forgetting grammar and vocabulary and relearning them is what cements them into the brain.[5] Spacing out revision is more effective than cramming – we know that, but students should also know that the space between revisiting material should vary depending on how far away the examination is. A cyclical approach is required. An examination 12 months away necessitates revisiting covered material about once a month. A test in 30 days should have topics revisited every 3 days – intervals of roughly a tenth of the time available.[6]

Summary

Students: the more tests and past questions you do, in an environment as close to examination conditions as possible, the better you are likely to perform on the day. If you prefer to listen to music while you revise, listen to songs in Spanish. However, tunes without any lyrics will be far less detrimental to your memory and retention, and silence is most effective.[5] If you choose to study with friends, choose carefully – effort is contagious.[7]

1. Mayer, R. E., & Anderson, R. B. (1991). Animations need narrations: An experimental test of dual-coding hypothesis. *Journal of Education Psychology*, (83)4, 484–490.
2. Roediger III, H. L., & Karpicke, J.D. (2006). Test-enhanced learning: Taking memory tests improves long-term retention. *Psychological Science*, 17(3), 249–255.
3. Nestojko, J., Bui, D., Kornell, N. & Bjork, E. (2014). Expecting to teach enhances learning and organisation of knowledge in free recall of text passages. *Memory and Cognition*, 42(7), 1038–1048.
4. Smith, A. M., Floerke, V. A., & Thomas, A. K. (2016) Retrieval practice protects memory against acute stress. *Science*, 354(6315), 1046–1048.
5. Perham, N., & Currie, H. (2014). Does listening to preferred music improve comprehension performance? *Applied Cognitive Psychology*, 28(2), 279–284.
6. Cepeda, N. J., Vul, E., Rohrer, D., Wixted, J. T. & Pashler, H. (2008). Spacing effects in learning a temporal ridgeline of optimal retention. *Psychological Science*, 19(11), 1095–1102.
7. Busch, B. & Watson, E. (2019), *The Science of Learning*, 1st ed. Routledge.

CONTENTS

The basics

Basic words and phrases 2
Phonics 5

Theme 1   People and lifestyle

Specification point

1.1   Introductions 8
1.1   Descriptions 10
1.1   Personality 12
1.1   Friendship 14
1.1   Relationships 16
1.1   Identity and relationships with others 18
1.2   Food and drink 20
1.2   Eating healthily 22
1.2   Being active 24
1.2   Aches and pains 26
1.2   Health resolutions 28
1.2   Healthy living and lifestyle 30
1.3   School and school subjects 32
1.3   School uniform and facilities 34
1.3   Options at age 16 36
1.3   The world of work 38
1.3   Looking for work 40
1.3   Education and work 42
        Key vocabulary 44
        Examination practice **45**

Theme 2 Popular culture

			☑
2.1	Activities at home	50	☐
2.1	Outdoor activities	52	☐
2.1	TV and cinema	54	☐
2.1	Making plans	56	☐
2.1	Past, present and future	58	☐
2.1	Free-time activities	60	☐
2.2	Celebrations	62	☐
2.2	Festivals around the world	64	☐
2.2	Special days	66	☐
2.2	Weddings	68	☐
2.2	Christmas time	70	☐
2.2	Customs, festivals and celebrations	72	☐
2.3	Celebrities	74	☐
2.3	Reality TV	76	☐
2.3	Celebrities as role models	78	☐
2.3	Influencers	80	☐
2.3	Pros and cons of fame	82	☐
2.3	Celebrity culture	84	☐
	Key vocabulary	86	☐
	Examination practice	**87**	☐

Theme 3 Communication and the world around us

			☑
3.1	Transportation	92	☐
3.1	The weather	94	☐
3.1	School holidays	96	☐
3.1	Holidays	98	☐
3.1	Places of interest	100	☐
3.1	Travel, tourism and places of interest	102	☐
3.2	Using a smartphone	104	☐
3.2	The internet	106	☐
3.2	Social media	108	☐
3.2	Technology problems	110	☐
3.2	The impact of technology	112	☐
3.2	Media and technology	114	☐
3.3	Where people live	116	☐
3.3	Towns and cities	118	☐
3.3	Describing the area	120	☐
3.3	The environment	122	☐
3.3	Our planet	124	☐
3.3	The environment and where people live	126	☐
	Key vocabulary	128	☐
	Examination practice	**129**	☐

Grammar

Nouns and articles	134 ☐
Adjectives	138 ☐
Adverbs	142 ☐
Pronouns	144 ☐
Verbs and tenses	148 ☐
Prepositions	158 ☐
Questions	159 ☐
Negation	160 ☐
Verb tables	161 ☐
Examination practice answers	167
Guidance on getting top marks	173
Index	181
Examination tips	**185**

Tiers, mark schemes and marking guidance

All of the higher tier exam practice questions in this book have been marked with an **H** symbol. Foundation level questions have been marked with an **F**. Boundary level questions may have both.

The answers to exam questions should be marked in accordance with the mark schemes published on the AQA website. A set of guidance notes on how to interpret the mark schemes for each question type on each paper can be downloaded from **ClearRevise.com**. This also contains advice and tips on how to gain as many marks as you can..

Understanding the specification reference tabs

This number refers to the Theme number.
In this example, **Theme 2: Popular culture**.

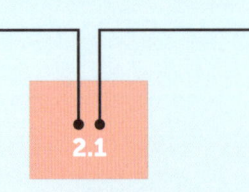

2.1

This number refers to the Topic number.
In this example, **Topic 1: Free-time activities**.

Downloading the speaking and listening clips

All of the MP3 clips can be downloaded from our website at **ClearRevise.com**.

A full copy of the **transcripts** is also available to download.

TRACK 1

Scan the **QR code** here or on each question with a **listening or speaking symbol**.

Then select the **track** indicated.

THE BASICS

No vocabulary is specified for KS2 or KS3 so this section includes some key words and phrases that students at all levels will find helpful. This book makes no assumptions about vocabulary previously taught.

The basics

BASIC WORDS AND PHRASES

Les jours de la semaine — The days of the week

lundi	mardi	mercredi	jeudi	vendredi	samedi	dimanche
Monday	*Tuesday*	*Wednesday*	*Thursday*	*Friday*	*Saturday*	*Sunday*

! In French, the days of the week do not have capital letters.

le weekend — *the weekend*

Useful phrases

l'année dernière	last year	mardi	on Tuesday
samedi dernier	last Saturday	le mardi	on Tuesdays
avant-hier	the day before yesterday	tous les vendredis	every Friday
hier	yesterday	tous les jours	everyday
hier matin	yesterday morning	le matin	in the morning
hier soir	yesterday evening	le soir	in the evening
aujourd'hui	today	ce soir	tonight
demain	tomorrow	la nuit	at night
demain après-midi	tomorrow afternoon	toujours	always
après-demain	the day after tomorrow	souvent	often
ce weekend	this weekend	parfois	sometimes
la semaine prochaine	next week	(ne ...) jamais	never

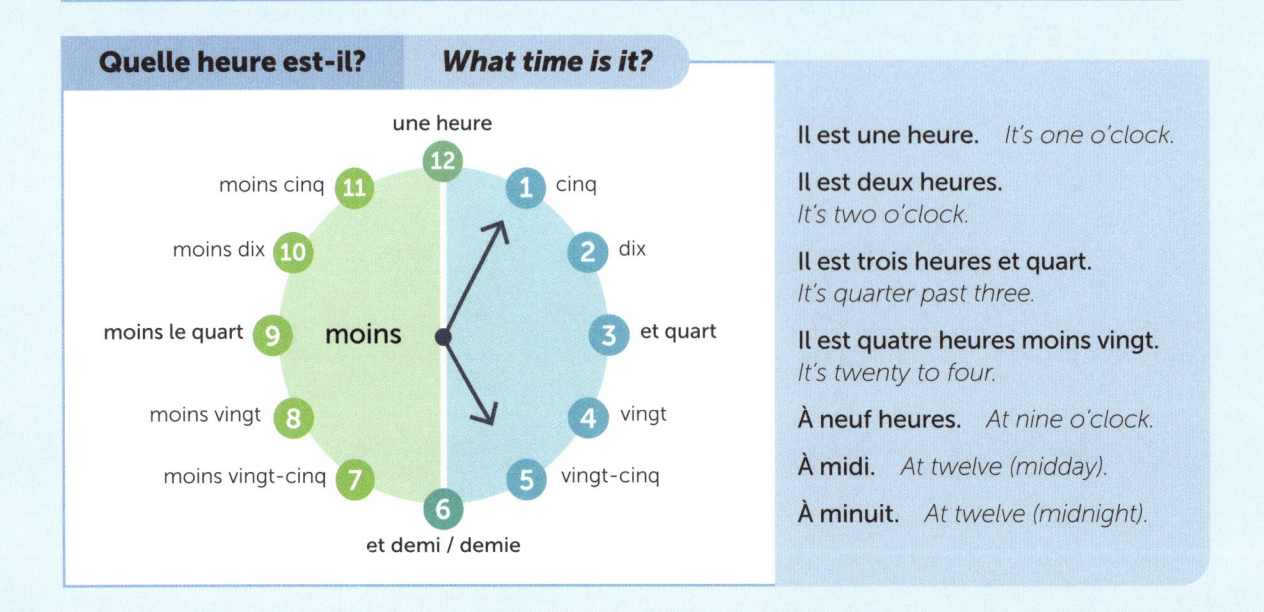

Quelle heure est-il? — What time is it?

Clock positions:
- 12 — une heure
- 1 — cinq
- 2 — dix
- 3 — et quart
- 4 — vingt
- 5 — vingt-cinq
- 6 — et demi / demie
- 7 — moins vingt-cinq
- 8 — moins vingt
- 9 — moins le quart
- 10 — moins dix
- 11 — moins cinq

moins

Il est une heure. *It's one o'clock.*

Il est deux heures. *It's two o'clock.*

Il est trois heures et quart. *It's quarter past three.*

Il est quatre heures moins vingt. *It's twenty to four.*

À neuf heures. *At nine o'clock.*

À midi. *At twelve (midday).*

À minuit. *At twelve (midnight).*

Les mois et les saisons — The months and seasons

janvier	février	mars
January	February	March

avril	mai	juin
April	May	June

juillet	août	septembre
July	August	September

octobre	novembre	décembre
October	November	December

! In French, the months of the year don't begin with a capital letter.

au printemps — *in spring*
en été — *in summer*
en automne — *in autumn*
en hiver — *in winter*

Mon anniversaire est en janvier.	My birthday is in January.
En été, on va à la plage.	In summer we go to the beach.
Aujourd'hui, c'est le 13 novembre.	Today is the 13th of November.
On fait toujours une fête le premier janvier.	We always have a party on the first of January.

Les nombres — Numbers

1	un	11	onze	21	vingt-et-un	40	quarante
2	deux	12	douze	22	vingt-deux	50	cinquante
3	trois	13	treize	23	vingt-trois	60	soixante
4	quatre	14	quatorze	24	vingt-quatre	70	soixante-dix
5	cinq	15	quinze	25	vingt-cinq	71	soixante-et-onze
6	six	16	seize	26	vingt-six	72	soixante-douze
7	sept	17	dix-sept	27	vingt-sept	80	quatre-vingts
8	huit	18	dix-huit	28	vingt-huit	81	quatre-vingt-un
9	neuf	19	dix-neuf	29	vingt-neuf	90	quatre-vingt-dix
10	dix	20	vingt	30	trente	91	quatre-vingt-onze

100	200	1000	2000	1 000 000
cent	deux-cents	mille	deux mille	un million

+ le premier/la première *first*   le/la deuxième *second*   le/la troisième *third*
en deux mille vingt-quatre – *in 2024*   en mille neuf-cent quatre-vingt-sept – *in 1987*
cinquante pour cent – *50%*   un quart – *a quarter*   un tiers – *a third*

AQA GCSE French | Basics

Les couleurs / *Colours*

marron brun brune *brown*	rouge *red*	jaune *yellow*	vert verte *green*	bleu bleue *blue*	blanc blanche *white*	gris grise *grey*	noir noire *black*

Greetings and being polite

Bonjour	*Hello / Hi*	Félicitations !	*Congratulations!*
Bonsoir	*Good evening (used from late afternoon onwards)*	S'il te plaît, S'il vous plaît	*Please (informal and formal)*
Bonne nuit	*Good night*	Merci	*Thank you*
Bienvenue	*Welcome*	D'accord	*Okay*
Ça va ?	*How are you?*	Pardon	*Sorry*
Au revoir	*Goodbye*	Monsieur	*Sir / Mr*
Bonne chance	*Good luck*	Madame	*Madam / Ms / Mrs*

Opinions

Introduce your opinion with **Je pense que**, **Je crois que**, **Je trouve que** *I think that* or **À mon avis** *In my opinion*. Then go on to express your ideas.

Joining words

parce que / car *because*	cependant *however*
alors *so*	mais *but*

Likes and dislikes

J'aime *I like*	Je n'aime pas *I don't like*	Je déteste *I hate*
Ça me plaît. *I like that.*	Ça ne me plaît pas. *I don't like that.*	

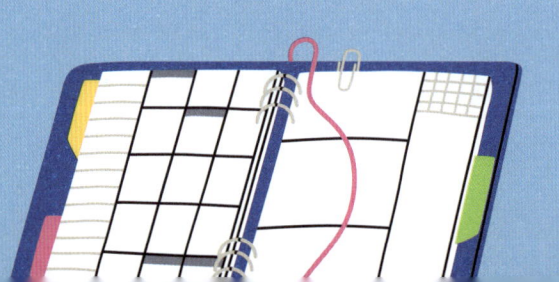

PHONICS

These are the most important French sounds. Listen to the recording and repeat.

Letter(s)	Sound	Examples
a	Open, like 'a' in *hat*.	avec
e	A short 'er' sound, like at the end of *butter*.	le, ne, de
é, er, ez	A bit like the English 'ay', but very short.	allé, aller, allez
è, ê, ai	Like the English 'e' in *egg*.	collège, bête, vrai
eu	Like the middle sound in *her*.	fleur, neuf
eu	More closed.	bleu, deux, veut
i, y	Like 'i' or a short 'ee' in English.	musique, gym
o	Open 'o', as in *not*.	porte
au, eau, o	Closed 'o', as *oh!*	sauf, beau
u	No exact match in English. Listen to the recording.	tu, bu, vu
ou	Like 'oo' in *look*.	sous, toujours
oi	Like a 'wah' sound.	toi, moi
oy	Like a 'wah' sound as above, followed by a 'ye' sound.	moyen, joyeux
en, an, em, am	A nasal vowel. Start with 'a', but the air escapes from the nose.	centre, grand, temps
on, om	A nasal vowel. Start with 'o', but the air escapes from the nose.	mon, tomber
ain, in, aim, im, ym	Another nasal vowel. Listen to the recording.	main, matin, faim, impossible, sympa
un	Another nasal vowel, very close in sound to 'ain'.	lundi
ch	Like the 'sh' sound at the end of *fish*.	chat, marché
c	Hard, like a 'k', when followed by 'a', 'o' or 'u'.	cadeau
c, ç	Soft, like an 's', when followed by 'e' or 'i', or with a cedilla: ç	ici, français
qu	Like a 'k' in English.	quel, banque
g	Hard, like 'g' in 'good', when followed by 'a', 'o' or 'u'.	gâteau
g	Soft like an English 'j', when followed by 'e' or 'i'.	manger, girafe
tion	Not like English '-tion'! Pronounce the 't' like an 's'.	attention
ien	Start with a 'ye', followed by an 'ain' nasal sound.	bien, chien
h	Don't make an English 'h' sound – it's silent in French.	hôpital
gn	A bit like the 'ny' sound in the English word 'onion'.	gagner, espagnol
r	Stronger than English 'r'. It comes from the back of the throat.	radio, regarde, France
s	Pronounced like a 'z', when between two vowels.	rose
s	Otherwise, like an 'ss' sound.	pense
th	Sounds like a normal 't'. Ignore the 'h'.	thé, maths, Thérèse
ill, ille, aill, ail	Usually, the 'll' is pronounced like 'ye' in English. Occasionally, the 'll' is pronounced like a normal 'l'.	fille, travaille ville, mille
Liaisons occur when, in two words that belong together, the first one ends in a consonant and the next one starts with a vowel or a silent **h**. The usually silent consonant is heard, running into the next word.		mon ami, vous avez, deux élèves, petit enfant

Anaïs et ses copains :

Mahmoud

Anaïs

Tommy

Lola

Hugo

You will see and hear Anaïs, Hugo, Lola, Mahmoud et Tommy regularly in this book. Enjoy their company!

TOPICS FOR THEME 1
People and lifestyle

Specification coverage

Topic 1   Identity and relationships with others
Topic 2   Healthy living and lifestyle
Topic 3   Education and work

Information about the four papers for Foundation (F) and Higher (H) tiers:

Paper 1 – Listening

Written exam:
35 minutes (F), 45 minutes (H)
40 marks (F), 50 marks (H)
25% of GCSE

The recording is controlled by the invigilator with built-in repetitions and pauses.

Each exam includes 5 minutes' reading time at the start of the question paper before the listening material is played and 2 minutes at the end of the recording to check your work.

Section A – Listening comprehension questions in English, to be answered in English or non-verbally ((F) 32 marks, (H) 40 marks).

Section B – Dictation where students transcribe 4 sentences ((F) 8 marks) or 5 sentences ((H) 10 marks).

Paper 2 – Speaking

Non-exam assessment (NEA):
7–9 minutes (F) or 10–12 minutes (H) +
15 minutes' supervised preparation time
50 marks, 25% of GCSE

Role play – 10 marks, 1–1.5 minutes. (F) (H)

Reading aloud passage and short conversation – 15 marks.
Recommended time 2–2.5 minutes (F) and 3–3.5 minutes (H).
Minimum 35 words (F) and minimum 50 words (H).

Photo card discussion (two photos) – 25 marks.
Photo card discussion time:
4–5 minutes (F) and 6–7 minutes (H).

Paper 3 – Reading

Written exam: 45 minutes (F), 1 hour (H)
50 marks, 25% of GCSE

Section A – Reading comprehension questions in English, to be answered in English or non-verbally (40 marks).

Section B – Translation from French into English, minimum of 35 words (F) or 50 words (H) (10 marks).

Paper 4 – Writing

Written exam: 1 hour 10 minutes (F),
1 hour 15 minutes (H)
50 marks, 25% of GCSE

Set of three short writing tasks. (F) only. 25 marks.

Translation of sentences from English into French, minimum 35 words (F), or 50 words (H) (10 marks).

Produce a piece of writing in response to three compulsory bullet points, approximately 90 words in total. Choose from two questions (15 marks). (F) (H)

Open-ended writing task.
Two compulsory bullet points, approximately 150 words in total. Choose from two questions. (25 marks). (H) only.

1.1

INTRODUCTIONS

Moi — *Me*

Here are four questions someone might ask when they want to get to know you.

Comment t'appelles-tu ?	What is your name?
Où habites-tu ?	Where do you live?
Quel âge as-tu ?	How old are you?
C'est quand, ton anniversaire ?	When is your birthday?

+
Comment ? means *how?*   (**Comment t'appelles-tu ?** means literally, *How do you call yourself?*)
Où ? means *where?*
Quel ? means *what?*   (**Quel âge as-tu ?** means literally, *What age have you?*)
Quand ? means *when?*
For more details about question words, go to **page 159**.

The first three questions in the list above use the most correct word order.

These alternatives are correct too, to ask the same things, but they are more informal:
Tu t'appelles comment ? Comment tu t'appelles ?
Tu habites où ? Où tu habites ?
Tu as quel âge ? Quel âge tu as ?

Your answers to the questions above will usually include the following phrases.

Je m'appelle ...	My name is ...
J'habite ...	I live ...
J'ai ... ans	I am ... years old
Mon anniversaire, c'est le ...	My birthday is on the ....

---

1. You hear a short interview with a French teenager. Choose the correct answers.   **TRACK 2**

   1.1 The person is called ...   **A** Lola.   **B** Noah.   **C** Ella.
   1.2 That person lives in ...   **A** Leeds.   **B** Nîmes.   **C** Lille.
   1.3 That person is ...   **A** 14 years old.   **B** 15 years old.   **C** 16 years old.
   1.4 That person's birthday is on the ... **A** 7th of March.   **B** 17th of May.   **C** 27th of May.

1.1 A   1.2 C   1.3 B   1.4 C

Questions et réponses — *Questions and answers*

When answering questions about yourself, try to include extra details.
Here are some examples.

Comment t'appelles-tu ?
Je m'appelle Dolorès, mais tout le monde m'appelle Lola.
My name is Dolorès, but everyone calls me Lola.

Où habites-tu ?
J'habite à Lille, dans le nord de la France.
I live in Lille, in the North of France.

Quel âge as-tu ?
J'ai quinze ans, mais je vais avoir seize ans la semaine prochaine.
I am fifteen but I am going to be sixteen next week.

C'est quand, ton anniversaire ?
Mon anniversaire, c'est le 27 mai. Je vais faire une fête.
My birthday is on the 27th of May. I am going to have a party.

2. How would you answer the four questions above? Prepare your answers and record yourself.

   2. Listen to the recording for a model answer.

   TRACK 3

+ Think of extra details you can add. Here are a few ideas you can adapt and use.

… et j'aime bien mon prénom.   *… and I quite like my name.*

… c'est un prénom d'origine écossaise / irlandaise / galloise / pakistanaise.
… it's a name of Scottish / Irish / Welsh / Pakistani origin.

… dans le centre de l'Angleterre / de l'Irlande du Nord / dans le sud de l'Écosse / dans le nord du pays de Galles.
… in the centre of England / of Northern Ireland / in the south of Scotland / in the north of Wales.

… car c'était mon anniversaire la semaine dernière.
… because it was my birthday last week.

… et j'adore faire la fête pour mon anniversaire.
… and I love having a party for my birthday.

1.1

DESCRIPTIONS

Ma famille et mes amis   *My family and friends*

Which of these words will you use to talk about your own family?

mon père *my father*	**ma mère** *my mother*	**mes grands-parents** *my grandparents*
mon frère (jumeau) *my (twin) brother*	**ma sœur (jumelle)** *my (twin) sister*	**mes demi-frères** *my half / stepbrothers*
mon beau-père *my stepfather*	**ma belle-mère** *my stepmother*	**mes cousins** *my cousins*

+

Just as there are three different words for *the* in French (**le**, **la**, **les**), there are three different words for *my*:

mon with a masculine singular noun

ma with a feminine singular noun

mes with a plural noun, masculine or feminine.

---

1. Listen to Anaïs talking about her younger brother, Lucas.

    1.1 Which of the following words do you hear? (They may not appear in the same order as the list.)

    TRACK 4

1	cheveux	*hair*		6	longs	*long*
2	blonds	*blond*		7	lunettes	*glasses*
3	bruns	*brown*		8	petit	*small*
4	courts	*short*		9	roux	*red*
5	grand	*tall*		10	yeux	*eyes*

    Listen again. Answer these questions.

    1.2 How old is Lucas?

    1.3 When is his birthday?

    1.4 What does he look like? Give **three** details.

    1.1 Words: 8, 1, 4, 10, 7.   1.2 10 years old   1.3 20 November
    1.4 short hair, blue eyes, wears glasses

! Adjectives (describing words) agree with the noun they describe. This means they usually end with an **e** if the adjective goes with a feminine noun, and an **s** for a plural noun. Some are slightly irregular: the feminine of **long** is **longue**, and **roux** changes to **rousse**.

For more details about adjectives, go to **pages 138-139**.

Avoir et être — *To have and to be*

2. You read these notes a writer made about the characters in her next book.

   2.1 Write **A** if only statement A is correct, **B** if only statement B is correct, **A + B** if both statements are correct.

   | Anaïs est très grande et elle a les cheveux longs. | Hugo est assez petit et il a les cheveux bruns. | Le petit chien de Lola s'appelle Tommy. | Tommy est brun avec un collier rouge. | Mahmoud a les cheveux frisés. |

Anaïs …	**A** is very tall.	**B** has long hair.
Hugo …	**A** is not very tall.	**B** has green eyes.
Lola's dog …	**A** is black.	**B** is called Tommy.
Mahmoud …	**A** has curly hair.	**B** has blond hair.

   2.2 👁 What is the colour of the dog's collar?

   2.1 Anaïs A + B, Hugo A, Lola's dog B, Mahmoud A.   2.2 Red.

Avoir, *to have*, and **être**, *to be*, are key verbs.
Make sure you know how to use them in the present tense:

avoir	être
j'ai	je suis
tu as	tu es
il / elle / on a	il / elle / on est
nous avons	nous sommes
vous avez	vous êtes
ils / elles ont	ils / elles sont

Don't forget to use the verb **avoir** when talking about age in French!

J'ai dix-sept ans. *I am 17 years old.* (or literally: *I have 17 years.*)

Use the verb **être** when stating your nationality, and add an **e** to the nationality adjective for a woman or girl.

Je suis …	anglaise / anglaise	écossais / écossaise	gallois / galloise	irlandais / irlandaise
I am …	*English*	*Scottish*	*Welsh*	*Irish*

3. Describe yourself or a member of your family using language from **pages 10–11**.

   3. Model response: Bonjour, je m'appelle Ludovic, mais tout le monde m'appelle Ludo. J'ai seize ans et je vais avoir dix-sept ans le weekend prochain. Je suis assez grand. J'ai les cheveux bruns, frisés et j'ai les yeux noirs. Mon chien s'appelle Toto. Il est blanc et noir et il porte un collier vert.

1.1

PERSONALITY

Ils sont comment ? — *What are they like?*

Here is a list of adjectives you may need to describe your friends.

amusant / amusante	*amusing, fun*	paresseux / paresseuse	*lazy*
compréhensif / compréhensive	*understanding*	sérieux / sérieuse	*serious*
désagréable	*unpleasant*	sportif / sportive	*sporty*
drôle	*funny*	sympa	*nice*
gentil / gentille	*kind*	timide	*shy*

! Remember that adjectives agree with the noun they describe. You usually need to add an **e** if the adjective goes with a feminine noun, and an **s** in the plural. Masculine adjectives ending in -eux do not change in the plural.

There are exceptions. If the adjective already ends in **e**, like **timide**, there is no need to add another **e**.

Sympa works for masculine or feminine, but you need to add an **s** in the plural: **sympas**.

Adjectives ending in **-eux** change to **-euse** in the feminine: **paresseux** (m), **paresseuse** (f).

Adjectives ending in **-if** change to **-ive** in the feminine: **sportif** (m), **sportive** (f).

Adjectives ending in **-il** change to **-ille** in the feminine: **gentil** (m), **gentille** (f). See **page 138**.

---

1. You read descriptions of four characters in a new book: Lola, Mahmoud, Anaïs and Hugo.

   > *Lola est sympa, et elle est drôle aussi.*
   > *Mahmoud est sportif et très généreux.*
   > *Anaïs est gentille, mais elle est paresseuse.*
   > *Hugo fait souvent des commentaires désagréables.*

   What do they think of each character?

   Write **P** for a positive opinion.

   Write **N** for a negative opinion.

   Write **P + N** for a positive and negative opinion.

   1. Lola P, Mahmoud P, Anaïs P + N, Hugo N

Des amis sportifs — *Sporty friends*

Most adjectives in French follow the noun they describe.

J'ai des **amis sympas**.	*I have **nice friends**.*
Lola préfère les **gens drôles**.	*Lola prefers **funny people**.*
Mahmoud a des **amis** très **sportifs**.	*Mahmoud has very **sporty friends**.*

+ For exceptions to this rule, see **page 101**.

Dictation

2. You will hear five statements about Anaïs and her friends. Listen carefully and write **one** word for each gap.

   You will hear each statement **three** times: the first time as a full statement, the second time in short sections and the third time again as a full statement.

   2.1 Anaïs a des amis très _____.

   2.2 Lola aime les histoires _____.

   2.3 Le _____ chien de Lola est très _____

   2.4 Mahmoud est _____ et il a des activités _____.

   2.5 Hugo est très _____, mais il n'est pas toujours _____.

   2.1. sympas   2.2 drôles   2.3 petit, amusant   2.4 sportif, intéressantes   2.5 intelligent, gentil

! Make sure any adjectives you write agree with their nouns.

Remember, if you hear a **t** at the end of a word, there must be an **e** afterwards, and maybe an **s** if it is plural. When there is a **t** at the very end of a word, it is silent.

To make comparisons, use the following words:

plus ... que/qu'... *more .../...-er than ...*	Lola est plus drôle qu'Hugo. *Lola is funnier than Hugo.*
moins que/qu' ... *less ... than...*	Anaïs est moins sportive que Mahmoud. *Anaïs is less sporty than Mahmoud.*
aussi ... que/qu' ... *as ... as ...*	Tommy est aussi amusant que Lola. *Tommy is as amusing as Lola.*

3. Translate these sentences into French.
   3.1 My friend is kinder than Hugo.
   3.2 Tommy is as funny as your dog.
   3.3 Lucas is smaller than my brother.
   3.4 Anaïs is less shy than her brother.

   3.1 Mon ami est plus gentil qu'Hugo.   3.2 Tommy est aussi drôle que ton chien.
   3.3 Lucas est plus petit que mon frère.   3.4 Anaïs est moins timide que son frère.

1.1

FRIENDSHIP

L'ami idéal / L'amie idéale — *The ideal friend*

Rewrite these phrases by order of importance for you.

L'ami idéal / L'amie idéale ...	The ideal friend ...
me fait rire.	*makes me laugh.*
me dit toujours la vérité.	*always tells me the truth.*
est toujours là pour moi.	*is always there for me.*
partage ses chocolats avec moi.	*shares their chocolates with me.*
aime la même musique que moi.	*likes the same music as me.*
m'écoute quand j'ai un problème.	*listens to me when I have a problem.*

Listen to Anaïs, Mahmoud and Lola giving their view on what makes the ideal friend.   TRACK 6

1. Which **two** aspects does each person mention? Write the correct letters.

   An ideal friend ...

A	makes me laugh.
B	is always there for me.
C	always tells me the truth.
D	likes the same music as me.
E	always listens to my problems.
F	shares their chocolates with me.

2. Listen to Lola again. What else does she say about her ideal friend?

   1. *Anaïs D, F, Mahmoud C, B, Lola E, A*
   2. *Lola says Tommy, her dog, is her ideal friend.*

+ When you want to say *me* with a verb (e.g. *tells me, makes me*), in French you use **me** (or **m'** before a vowel or a silent h) and put it before the verb.
Elle me fait rire. Elle me dit la vérité. Elle m'écoute.

When *me* goes with a preposition (*with me, for me*) or with 'as' or 'than', use **moi**.
Elle est toujours là pour moi. Elle aime la même musique que moi.

The same rule applies to *you*: use **te / t'** with a verb and **toi** with a preposition.
Elle te fait rire et elle partage ses chocolats avec toi.

For more about object pronouns and emphatic pronouns, see **pages 105 and 146**.

J'aime et tu détestes — *I like and you hate*

You have, by now, come across several **-er** verbs, such as **aimer**, **écouter**, **détester** and **habiter**.

All regular **-er** verbs follow the same pattern of endings in the present tense.

détester
je déteste
tu détestes
il / elle / on déteste
nous détestons
vous détestez
ils / elles détestent

! See **page 149** for more details.

Remember to drop the **e** of **je** when the next word starts with a vowel or a silent **h**.

j'aime   j'adore   j'écoute   j'habite

Note that verbs ending in **-ger**, like **partager**, need an extra **e** in the **nous** form, after the **g** and before the usual **-ons** ending.

nous partageons

Similarly, verbs ending in **-cer**, like **commencer**, need a cedilla under the **c** (**ç**) in the **nous** form, before the usual **-ons** ending.

nous commençons

---

3. Read this interview with twins Lolo and Lulu and add the endings to complete the verbs.

3.1 Journaliste: Tu aim_____ avoir une sœur jumelle, Lolo ?

3.2 Lolo: Oui, j'ador_____ ma sœur jumelle !
Lulu: Moi aussi !

3.3 Journaliste: Vous partag_____ une chambre ?

3.4 Lolo et Lulu: Oui, nous partag_____ une chambre.
Journaliste: C'est bien ?

3.5 Lolo: Oui, car Lulu écout_____ la même musique que moi.

3.6 Lulu: On aim_____ les mêmes choses !
Journaliste: Vous avez deux frères ?

3.7 Lolo: Oui, mais ils n'aim_____ pas les mêmes choses …

3.8 Lulu: … et ils n'écout_____ pas la même musique.

3.1 aimes   3.2 adore   3.3 partagez   3.4 partageons   3.5 écoute   3.6 aime   3.7 aiment   3.8 écoutent

1.1

RELATIONSHIPS

On s'entend bien — *We get on well*

Some of the verbs you need to talk about family and friend relationships are reflexive verbs.

s'amuser	to have a good time
se disputer	to argue with
s'entendre avec	to get on with
s'intéresser à	to be interested in
se ressembler	to look alike, to look like each other

! Reflexive verbs need an extra pronoun (**me**, **te**, etc.) for each person of the verb:

je **me** dispute		je **m'**amuse
tu **te** disputes		tu **t'**amuses
il/elle/on **se** dispute		il/elle/on **s'**amuse
nous **nous** disputons		nous **nous** amusons
vous **vous** disputez		vous **vous** amusez
ils/elles **se** disputent		ils/elles **s'**amusent

If the verb starts with a vowel or a silent h, drop the **e** of **me**, **te** and **se** and replace it with an apostrophe. For more details about reflexive verbs, go to **page 155**.

1. Translate these sentences into **English**.
    1.1 Je m'entends bien avec ma famille.
    1.2 Je me dispute rarement avec mes amis.
    1.3 Mon frère et moi, on se ressemble beaucoup.
    1.4 Mes parents sont divorcés, mais ils s'entendent bien.
    1.5 Généralement, nous nous intéressons aux mêmes choses.

1.1 I get on well with my family.   1.2 I rarely argue with my friends.   1.3 My brother and I look very much alike.   1.4 My parents are divorced, but they get on well.   1.5 We are generally interested in the same things.

+ Look out for any phrases you can adapt and learn, ready to use when you write about yourself.

On se dispute …   *We argue …*

2. Listen to Anaïs talking about her relationship with her siblings. Answer the questions.
   - 2.1 Who does she get on with? Why?
   - 2.2 Who does she have a more difficult relationship with?
   - 2.3 Why do they argue?

   2.1 With her younger brother, because they have the same sense of humour.
   2.2 With her older sister. 2.3 Because they are not interested in the same things.

3. Read aloud the following text, then listen to the recording to check your pronunciation.

   > Mes parents sont divorcés et je m'entends bien avec ma mère et mon beau-père.
   >
   > Par contre, je me dispute souvent avec mes deux frères jumeaux. Ils sont gentils, mais ils font beaucoup de bruit.
   >
   > Ma cousine est fille unique, alors c'est plus calme chez elle.

   ! Remember that words that look like English words usually sound different in French. Listen out for the French pronunciation of **dispute** and **unique**.

   Pay attention to the pronunciation of **chez elle**. As the two words belong together and the second word starts with a vowel, both words are said without a pause and the **z** is pronounced.

4. Translate the reading aloud paragraph in Q3 into **English**.

   4. My parents are divorced, and I get on well with my mother and my stepfather. On the other hand, I often argue with my twin brothers. They are kind, but they make a lot of noise. My cousin is an only child, so it is quieter at her place.

   + Always make sure you understand everything you read. Then make a note of useful phrases so you can adapt and re-use them for your own writing and speaking tasks.

1.1

IDENTITY AND RELATIONSHIPS WITH OTHERS

Assemblage — *Putting it all together*

1. **F** Choose the correct French word from the three options in the grid.
   This type of exercise appears in the Foundation Writing exam only.

   1.1 Je _____ irlandaise.
       ai sommes suis

   1.2 Ma sœur _____ les cheveux longs.
       a avoir est

   1.3 Mes frères jumeaux _____ douze ans.
       avoir ont sont

   1.4 Mes parents _____ très compréhensifs.
       est être sont

   1.5 Est-ce que tu _____ le sens de l'humour ?
       as ont sont

   ! If your answers were not all correct, have another look at **page 11**, then redo the exercise.

2. You are writing an email to introduce yourself to a new penfriend in France.
   Write approximately **90 words** in **French**.
   You must write something about each bullet point.

   Mention:
   - your name, where you live and what you look like
   - your age and your birthday
   - some other detail about your family.

   1.1 suis 1.2 a 1.3 ont 1.4 sont 1.5 as

   2. Model response:

   Bonjour ! Je m'appelle Shamik, mais tout le monde m'appelle Mik. J'habite à Durham, dans le nord de l'Angleterre. Je suis assez grand, j'ai les cheveux bruns et les yeux bleus.

   J'ai quinze ans, mais je vais avoir seize ans le mois prochain. Mon anniversaire, c'est le 13 novembre. Je vais faire une grande fête avec tous mes amis.

   J'habite avec mon père et ma mère. Généralement, je m'entends bien avec ma famille, parce que nous avons le sens de l'humour. C'est très important !

Photo card

3. Look at the photo and make notes about what you can say about it. Then set a timer and talk about it for about 45 seconds. Record yourself if possible. At the end, listen to the recording for a model answer.

TRACK 9

! Once you have listened to the model answer, look at the transcription online. Make a note of useful words and phrases, then have another go.

Role play

4. Use what you have learned to prepare what you would say in this role play scenario.

    You are talking to a French-speaking friend about friendship.
    Your friend will speak first.

    When you see this —?— you will have to ask a question.

    4.1 Say something about your best friend. (Give **one** detail.)

    4.2 Say why you like them. (Give **two** details.)

    4.3 Say why you get on well. (Give **two** details.)

    4.4 Mention **one** thing you do together.

    ? 4.5 Ask your French-speaking friend a question about friendship.

    Now listen to the audio for a model response.

TRACK 10

! You should address your friend as **tu**.

AQA GCSE French | Theme 1

19

FOOD AND DRINK

Manger et boire — *Eating and drinking*

1. You hear an interview about Lola's likes and dislikes.
   For each question, which **two** items are mentioned? Write the correct letters.

A	fish
B	ice cream
C	meat
D	tea
E	vegetables
F	water

   TRACK 11

   1.1 E, A   1.2 F, D

To talk about your likes and dislikes and preferences, start with the following verbs.

j'adore	j'aime	je n'aime pas	je déteste	je préfère
I love	*I like*	*I don't like*	*I hate*	*I prefer*

Here is a list of some food and drinks.

l'alcool	alcohol		le fruit	fruit		le pain	bread
le café	coffee		le gâteau	cake		le poisson	fish
l'eau	water		la glace	ice cream		le thé	tea
les frites	chips		le lait	milk		la viande	meat
le fromage	cheese		les légumes	vegetables		le vin	wine

> **+** To learn and remember those words, rewrite them as two lists: one for food (**la nourriture**) and another for drinks (**les boissons**). And write them out again! This time, one list of what you like (**j'aime …**) and another of what you don't like (**je n'aime pas …**).
>
> Test yourself. Hide the English to make sure you know the meaning of each item. Then hide the French to make sure you know the French word. Also make sure you know whether you need **le** (for masculine singular), or **la** (for feminine singular).

Note how to introduce a noun describing a filling or a flavour:

au	with a masculine singular noun	un sandwich au fromage
à la	with a feminine singular noun	une glace à la vanille
à l'	with a noun starting with a vowel	un gâteau à l'ananas
aux	with a plural noun	une pizza aux champignons

Tu aimes ou tu n'aimes pas ?   *Do you like it or not?*

2. Read aloud the following text in **French**, then listen to the recording.

   > Au petit-déjeuner, je prends du thé et du pain. Au déjeuner, je choisis souvent un sandwich au fromage et un fruit. Le soir, on dîne en famille. On mange généralement de la viande avec des légumes et on boit de l'eau.

   For extra practice, translate that reading aloud text into **English**.

   2. *For breakfast, I have tea and bread. For lunch, I often choose a cheese sandwich and some fruit. In the evening, we have dinner as a family. We usually eat meat with vegetables and drink water.*

! Remember not to pronounce the **d** or the **s** at the end of **prends**.

The same rule applies to the final **s** and **t** of **choisis**, **fruit**, **légumes** and **boit**. Also take care with the pronunciation of short words like **du**, **de la** and **des**. Listen to the recording several times, to help you practise.

After verbs of likes and dislikes (such as **j'aime**, **j'adore**, **je déteste**), use **le**, **la** or **les**.
After other verbs (such as **je mange**, **je bois**, **je prends**), use **du**, **de l'**, **de la** or **des**.

j'aime	je prends
le pain	du pain
la viande	de la viande
l'eau	de l'eau
les frites	des frites

3. Translate these sentences into **French**.
   3.1 I hate fish, but I love chips.
   3.2 Do you like mushroom pizza?
   3.3 My stepfather doesn't like coffee, so he's having tea.
   3.4 I don't like meat, so I am choosing vegetables and cheese.

   3.1 Je déteste le poisson, mais j'aime beaucoup les frites.   3.2 Tu aimes les pizzas aux champignons ?   3.3 Mon beau-père n'aime pas le café, alors il prend du thé.   3.4 Je n'aime pas la viande, alors je choisis des légumes et du fromage.

Make sure you know the present tense forms of these high frequency verbs.

prendre *to take*	**boire** *to drink*	**choisir** *to choose*
je prend**s**	je boi**s**	je choisi**s**
tu prend**s**	tu boi**s**	tu choisi**s**
il / elle / on pren**d**	il / elle / on boi**t**	il / elle / on choisi**t**
nous pren**ons**	nous buv**ons**	nous chois**issons**
vous pren**ez**	vous buv**ez**	vous chois**issez**
ils / elles prenn**ent**	ils / elles boiv**ent**	ils / elles chois**issent**

! See **page 149** for more about present tense endings.

AQA GCSE French | Theme 1

1.2

EATING HEALTHILY

C'est bon pour la santé ? — Is it healthy?

1. Anaïs and her friends are saying what they eat and don't eat.

   Je mange souvent du fromage, mais je ne mange pas de viande. — Anaïs

   Je mange des légumes tous les jours. Je ne mange jamais de fromage, car je suis allergique aux produits laitiers. — Hugo

   Je mange de la viande, du poisson, des légumes, du fromage. Je ne suis pas difficile ! — Mahmoud

   Match the correct person with each of the following questions.
   Write **A** for Anaïs, **H** for Hugo, **M** for Mahmoud.
   1.1 Who eats vegetables every day?
   1.2 Who is clearly not vegetarian?
   1.3 Who never eats cheese?
   1.4 Who doesn't eat meat?
   1.5 ❶ Read Hugo's answer again. What is the meaning of 'allergique aux produits laitiers'?

   1.1 H   1.2 M   1.3 H   1.4 A   1.5 allergic to dairy products

To say what you don't do or how often you do something, use the following words and phrases.

ne … pas	not
ne … plus ❶	not any more
ne … jamais	never
parfois	sometimes
souvent	often
tous les jours	every day
une fois / deux fois par semaine	once / twice a week

+ To memorise these, use each one in a short sentence about your own eating preferences, and learn them. You can adapt and re-use phrases by Anaïs, Hugo and Mahmoud above.

22 ClearRevise

Qu'est-ce que tu ne manges pas ? — *What do you not eat?*

When you're talking about likes and dislikes, you use **le**, **la**, **l'** or **les** before a noun (see **page 21**). With other verbs, such as saying what you have or what you take, it's **du**, **de la**, **de l'**, **des**. But with a negative verb (**ne ... pas**), just use **de**. Shorten it to **d'** before a vowel.

je prends	je ne prends pas
du pain	de pain
de la glace	de glace
de l'eau	d'eau
des frites	de frites

2. Now use and practise that grammar knowledge in this gap fill task.
   Complete the following sentences in **French**.
   Choose the correct word from the three options.

   2.1 Je ne mange jamais _____ frites.
       de   du   des

   2.2 Il prend _____ viande tous les jours.
       de   d'   de la

   2.3 Sa mère ne boit pas souvent _____ alcool.
       de   d'   de l'

   2.4 🄷 Tu ne manges plus _____ gâteaux ?
       des   du   de

   2.1 de   2.2 de la   2.3 d'   2.4 🄷 de

Dictation

3. You will hear **five** sentences, repeated **three** times (the first time as a full sentence, the second time in short sections and the third time again as a full sentence).
   Write them down in **French**.

   3.1 Je ne bois jamais de vin.   3.2 Il boit parfois du thé.
   3.3 Tu manges souvent des fruits ?   3.4 Mon frère ne prend jamais de fromage.
   3.5 🄷 Vous mangez des gâteaux une fois par semaine ?

> **!** Note that on the Foundation paper **F**, there are only **four** sentences.

> **+** Make sure you understand each sentence, so you can re-use them in your own speaking and writing.
> Here is a translation: 3.1 I never drink wine.   3.2 He sometimes drinks tea.   3.3 Do you often eat fruit?   3.4 My brother never has cheese.   3.5 🄷 Do you eat cakes once a week?

AQA GCSE French | Theme 1

1.2

BEING ACTIVE

Pour garder la forme *To stay in shape*

1. Anaïs and her friends are saying what sports they practise.

   Je vais parfois à la piscine avec mes copines. C'est tout. Je ne fais pas beaucoup de sport, car je n'aime pas ça. — Anaïs

   Pour garder la forme, je joue au basket dans l'équipe de mon collège. C'est sympa ! — Lola

   Je fais de l'athlétisme et de la natation deux fois par semaine. J'aime aussi jouer au foot. J'adore le sport, même quand je ne gagne pas ! — Mahmoud

   Complete the sentences. Write the letter for the correct option.
   1.1 Anaïs … **A** doesn't like sports much.   **B** loves swimming.   **C** likes all sports.
   1.2 Lola is in her school basketball team, and … **A** she finds it difficult.   **B** she likes winning.   **C** she likes it.
   1.3 Mahmoud goes swimming … **A** after football.   **B** twice a week.   **C** twice a month.
   1.4 🄷 Read Mahmoud's final sentence again. He says: **même quand je ne gagne pas !** What does that mean?

   1.1 A   1.2 C   1.3 B   1.4 🄷 even when I don't win.

Aller, *to go*, and **faire**, *to do/make*, are two verbs you will need frequently.

As they are very irregular, make sure you know how to conjugate them in the present tense.

aller	faire
je vais	je fais
tu vas	tu fais
il / elle / on va	il / elle / on fait
nous allons	nous faisons
vous allez	vous faites
ils / elles vont	ils / elles font

Tu as joué au foot hier ?   *Did you play football yesterday?*

Remember the difference between the two main past tenses:
the perfect tense (**passé composé**) and the imperfect tense (**imparfait**).

The perfect tense is in two parts: the auxiliary (usually **avoir** in the present tense) + the past participle of the verb you want to use. Use the perfect tense to say what you, or someone else, did in the past.
J'<u>ai joué</u> au foot samedi dernier. *I played football last Saturday.*

The endings of the imperfect tense are: **-ais, -ais, -ait, -ions, -iez, -aient**. Use this tense to describe what it was like in the past, or what you, or someone else, were doing. You can also use it to talk about what you, or someone else, used to do regularly.

C'<u>était</u> super ! *It was great!*
Je <u>jouais</u> avec mon chien quand tu as appelé. *I was playing with my dog when you called me.*
Quand j'<u>étais</u> petite, j'<u>aimais</u> faire du trampoline. *When I was small, I used to like trampolining.*

> **+** Turn to **page 150** for more details about the perfect and imperfect tenses.

---

2. Underline the verbs in these sentences. Circle the **one** verb that is an infinitive.
   Write down whether the verbs are in the present, perfect or the imperfect tenses.
   Then translate the sentences into **English**.

   2.1 Hier, j'ai joué au basket.
   2.2 En ce moment, je fais du judo.
   2.3 C'était super à la piscine le weekend dernier.
   2.4 Quand j'étais petit, j'aimais courir avec mon chien.

   2.1 ai joué, perfect tense   2.2 fais, present   2.3 était, imperfect   2.4 étais, imperfect; aimais, imperfect; courir, infinitive

   Translations: 2.1 Yesterday I played basketball.   2.2 At the moment, I am doing judo.
   2.3 It was great at the swimming pool last weekend.   2.4 When I was little, I used to like running with my dog.

---

3. Translate these sentences into **French**.
   3.1 My team won yesterday.
   3.2 I was playing with my brother.
   3.3 Last week, we played basketball at school.
   3.4 My sister used to go to the swimming pool twice a week.
   3.5 When I was ten, I used to like drinking milk for breakfast.

   3.1 Mon équipe a gagné hier.   3.2 Je jouais avec mon frère.   3.3 La semaine dernière, on a joué au basket au collège.   3.4 Ma sœur allait à la piscine deux fois par semaine.
   3.5 Quand j'avais dix ans, j'aimais boire du lait au petit-déjeuner.

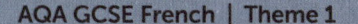

1.2

ACHES AND PAINS

Tu as mal où ? *Where does it hurt?*

1. You hear four people with different health problems. Where does it hurt? Write the correct letter.

   TRACK 14

A	arm
B	ears
C	eyes
D	feet
E	hand
F	head

   1.1 F   1.2 D   1.3 C   1.4 B

le bras	arm	la jambe	leg	la peau	skin
les cheveux (m pl)	hair	la main	hand	le pied	foot
le corps	body	l'œil ❶ (m)	eye	la tête	head
le dos	back	l'oreille	ears	les yeux (m pl)	eyes

+ To help you memorise these words, draw an outline of a person and label each part.

To talk about where it hurts or where you have a pain or an ache, start with **J'ai mal …**

What comes next depends on whether the noun you're going to mention is masculine or feminine, starts with a vowel, or is plural.

	Example	Use	
masculine singular	le dos	au	J'ai mal au dos *I have backache*
feminine singular	la tête	à la	J'ai mal à la tête *I have a headache*
masculine or feminine singular starting with a vowel	l'oreille	à l'	J'ai mal à l'oreille *I have a pain in my ear*
all plurals	les pieds	aux	J'ai mal aux pieds *My feet hurt*

Un rendez-vous chez le médecin — *A doctor's appointment*

Some verbs make the perfect tense with **être** instead of **avoir** as the auxiliary.

Aller, *to go*, **tomber**, *to fall*, and **se blesser**, *to injure oneself*, are three of those verbs.

Je <u>suis allé</u> à la piscine ce matin. *I went to the swimming pool this morning.*
Il <u>est tombé</u> de vélo lundi dernier. *He fell off his bike last Monday.*
Elle <u>s'est blessée</u> à la main hier soir. *She injured her hand last night.*

+ For more details about the perfect tense with **être**, go to **page 150**.

---

2. Translate these sentences into **English**.

   2.1 Je suis très fatigué et j'ai mal à la tête.
   2.2 Il est allé chez le médecin, car il était malade.
   2.3 Elle est tombée de vélo, mais ce n'est pas grave.
   2.4 Tu as mal aux pieds parce que tu as trop marché hier.
   2.5 🄷 Elle est à l'hôpital car elle s'est blessée à la jambe.

2.1 I am very tired and I have a headache. 2.2 He went to the doctor's because he was ill. 2.3 She fell off her bike, but it's not serious. 2.4 Your feet hurt because you walked too much yesterday. 2.5 🄷 She is in hospital because she injured her leg.

Role play

3. Use what you have learned to prepare what you would say in this role play scenario. You are talking to your friend. Your friend will speak first.
   When you see this **–?–** you will have to ask a question.

   3.1 Say you went to the doctor's this morning.
   3.2 Describe your symptoms. (Give **two** details.)
   3.3 Say it is not serious.
   3.4 Give a reason for the way you are feeling.
   ? 3.5 Ask your friend a question about their health.

   Now listen to the audio for a model response.

TRACK 15

⭐ In order to score full marks in the exam, you must include a verb in all five things you say.

You should address your friend as **tu**.

AQA GCSE French | Theme 1

1.2

HEALTH RESOLUTIONS

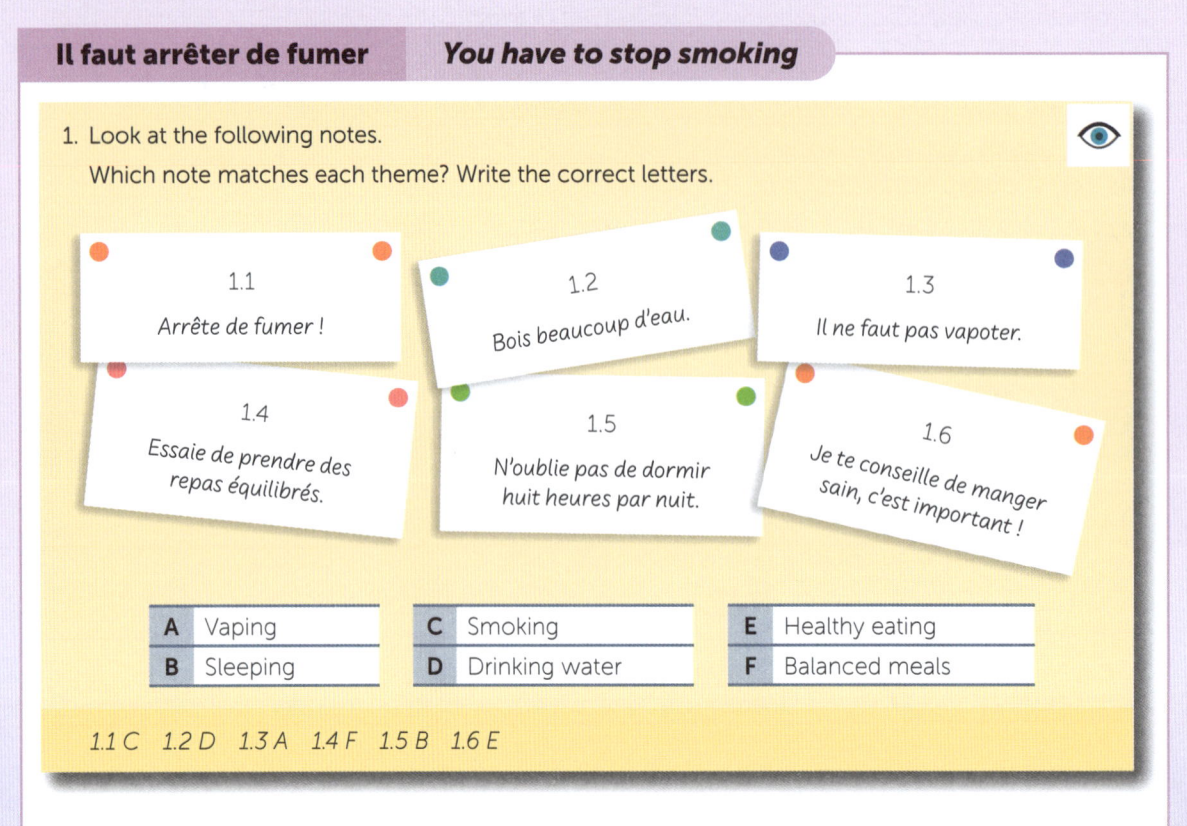

Il faut arrêter de fumer *You have to stop smoking*

1. Look at the following notes.
   Which note matches each theme? Write the correct letters.

   1.1 Arrête de fumer !

   1.2 Bois beaucoup d'eau.

   1.3 Il ne faut pas vapoter.

   1.4 Essaie de prendre des repas équilibrés.

   1.5 N'oublie pas de dormir huit heures par nuit.

   1.6 Je te conseille de manger sain, c'est important !

A	Vaping
B	Sleeping
C	Smoking
D	Drinking water
E	Healthy eating
F	Balanced meals

   1.1 C   1.2 D   1.3 A   1.4 F   1.5 B   1.6 E

To tell someone what to do or not to do, you can use **il faut / il ne faut pas** + infinitive.
Il faut dormir ! *You must sleep.*
Il ne faut pas fumer. *You must not smoke.*

You can also use the imperative form of the verb. To do that, start from the present tense, remove the pronoun (**tu**) and remove the final **-s** if it is an **-er** verb.

Present tense	Imperative
tu arrêtes *you stop*	arrête *stop*
tu évites *you avoid*	évite *avoid*
tu ne bois pas *you don't drink*	ne bois pas *don't drink*

! Also remember to use a verb in the infinitive after **de**.
N'oublie pas de boire. *Don't forget to drink.*
Essaie de manger sain. *Try to eat healthily.*
Je te conseille de dormir. *I advise you to sleep.*

Mes bonnes résolutions — *My good resolutions*

To say what you are going to do in the future, start with **je vais**, I am going to, followed by a verb in the infinitive.

Je vais boire plus d'eau. *I am going to drink more water.*

Alternatively, say what you would like to do, starting with **je voudrais**, followed by an infinitive.

Je voudrais être en bonne santé. *I would like to be healthy.*

2. Read aloud the following text, then listen to the recording to check your pronunciation.

TRACK 16

> Le médecin m'a conseillé de manger moins gras. Alors, je vais éviter de prendre trop de frites. Je vais aussi choisir moins de desserts sucrés. En plus, je voudrais dormir plus de sept heures par nuit. Avec tout ça, je vais être en bonne santé ?

For extra practice, translate that reading aloud text into **English**.

2. The doctor has advised me to eat less fat. So I am going to avoid having too many chips. I am also going to choose fewer sweet desserts. In addition, I would like to sleep more than seven hours a night. With all that, am I going to be healthy?

You can use **moins** and **plus** (*less* and *more*) with an adjective:

moins sucré	less sweet
plus sain	healthier

If you use **moins** or **plus** with a noun, add **de** before the noun (**d'** if it starts with a vowel).

moins de sucre	less sugar
plus d'eau	more water

Trop follows the same pattern.

trop gras	too greasy
trop de frites	too many chips

3. Write a note to yourself about making your diet more healthy.
   Write approximately **90 words** in **French**. You must write something about each bullet point. Mention:
   - foods to eat more or less of
   - changes in what you drink
   - something else you would like to do.

3. Model answer: Voici mes nouvelles résolutions pour être en bonne santé. D'abord, je vais essayer de manger plus de fruits et légumes et moins de plats gras, comme les frites et les hamburgers. Je vais aussi éviter de choisir des desserts trop sucrés.

En plus, je sais qu'il faut boire beaucoup d'eau, alors je vais faire ça. Les boissons sucrées, ça va de temps en temps, mais pas trop souvent.

Enfin, je crois que je ne dors pas assez. Je voudrais essayer de dormir huit heures par nuit. Bonne chance, moi !

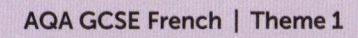

AQA GCSE French | Theme 1

1.2

HEALTHY LIVING AND LIFESTYLE

Assemblage   *Putting it all together*

1. You hear this podcast, with Mimi, a sports champion.

   Answer the questions in **English**.

   1.1 What is Mimi's sport?
   1.2 How do we know Mimi is in good health?
   1.3 What types of food does Mimi eat every day?
   1.4 What does Mimi say about drinking alcohol and smoking?
   1.5 How many hours of sleep does Mimi recommend?

   Choose the correct answer.

   1.6 **H** What is Mimi's comment about her grandmother's chocolate cake?

        A She avoids it.
        B It's irresistible.
        C She makes it when she wins a race.

   TRACK 17

   Once you have completed this listening task, turn to the transcript online. Make a note of all the key language that you would like to be able to re-use in your own speaking and writing tasks.

   1.1 swimming.   1.2 She says she isn't often ill.   1.3 Fruit and vegetables.   1.4 She doesn't drink alcohol, and her advice is for listeners to stop smoking now.   1.5 8 hours a night.   1.6 B

2. Your friend has sent you an email about their food and drink preferences.

   > Je n'aime pas la viande, je suis végétarienne, mais j'adore les légumes et le fromage.
   >
   > D'habitude, au petit-déjeuner, je prends des céréales et je bois du thé. Aujourd'hui, à midi, je vais manger un sandwich au fromage et un yaourt à l'ananas.
   >
   > Hier soir, au dîner, j'ai mangé une pizza aux champignons et une glace à la vanille. C'était délicieux ! Et toi ? Qu'est-ce que tu aimes et qu'est-ce que tu n'aimes pas ?

   Your turn! Answer your friend's email. Write approximately **90 words** in **French**. Describe:

   - what you like and don't like
   - what you ate last night
   - how you would like to change your diet.

   2. *Model answer: Moi, je ne suis pas végétarienne, car j'adore la viande. J'aime aussi les légumes et le fromage, mais je déteste le poisson. Hier soir, au restaurant, mes parents ont choisi du poisson avec des frites. Moi, je n'ai pas pris de poisson, j'ai mangé du poulet aux tomates. C'était très bon ! Moi aussi j'aime la glace à la vanille. En fait, j'adore les desserts et les gâteaux au chocolat, mais je vais essayer de manger moins de sucre et plus de fruits. Je veux être en bonne santé.*

Photo card

3. Look at the photo and make notes about it. Then set a timer and talk about it for about **45 seconds**. At the end, listen to the recording for a model answer.

> **+** To prepare for this task, have another look at all the language in this topic and adapt it.

4. Listen to the audio and answer the **four** questions in **French** related to healthy living and lifestyle. Pause after each question to give your response.

   4. Listen to the audio for a model response. Think about the answers you gave and have another go to help you improve.

+ Try to answer all questions as fully as you can. For example:
- **Tu manges souvent des légumes ?**
- **Oui, je mange des légumes tous les jours, car c'est bon pour la santé.**

Or:
- **Oui, je mange beaucoup de légumes. En fait, je voudrais essayer de devenir végétarien/végétarienne.**

AQA GCSE French | Theme 1

SCHOOL AND SCHOOL SUBJECTS

Au collège — **At school**

1. You hear an interview about Hugo's school week.
   Choose the correct answer and write the letter. *TRACK 19*

1.1	Hugo's favourite day of the week is …	**A** Monday.	**B** Wednesday.	**C** Saturday.
1.2	Hugo finds his history teacher is …	**A** very interesting.	**B** quite boring.	**C** unfriendly.
1.3	Hugo's least favourite subject is …	**A** Maths.	**B** Physics.	**C** Biology.
1.4	On Saturdays, Hugo has English and …	**A** IT.	**B** PE.	**C** Maths.

   Answer this question in **English**.
   1.5 Why does Hugo find lessons difficult on Saturdays?

   1.1 B   1.2 A   1.3 C   1.4 A   1.5 because he is tired.

! If you need to revise days of the week in French, go to **page 2**.

Also remember the difference between **le lundi** and **lundi** (or any other day of the week).
Le lundi means *on Mondays*. **Lundi** means *on Monday*, meaning *this Monday*.

Don't translate the English word *on* in this context.
J'ai français le lundi et le mercredi. *I have French on Mondays and Wednesdays.*

Check you know your school subjects in French:

l'anglais *English*	**l'espagnol** *Spanish*	**le français** *French*	**l'informatique** *IT*
la biologie *biology*	**la physique** *physics*	**la géographie** *geography*	**l'EPS** *PE*
	les maths *maths*	**l'histoire** *history*	

+ If you are talking about likes and dislikes, use the direct article **le**, **la**, **l'**, or **les**.
J'aime la biologie, je déteste l'histoire, je préfère les maths.
I like biology, I hate history, I prefer maths.

There is no need for **le/la/l'/les** when talking about a specific lesson or teacher, but pay attention to the word order. Use **de**, or **d'** in front of a vowel or a silent h, directly followed by the name of the school subject.
J'ai un cours de maths le lundi. *I have a maths lesson on Mondays.*
J'aime bien ma prof d'informatique. *I quite like my IT teacher.*

Mon emploi du temps — My timetable

Check you know these key verbs so that you talk about your school day.

arriver	to arrive
finir	to finish
manger	to eat
commencer	to start
rentrer à la maison	to go home
se lever	to get up
se réveiller	to wake up

+ To remember these words, rewrite them in the right chronological order for you.

For a reminder of how to say the time, go to **page 2**.

---

2. Translate these sentences into **English**.

   2.1 Le matin, je me réveille à sept heures.

   2.2 D'habitude, j'arrive au collège à huit heures et quart.

   2.3 Le premier cours commence à neuf heures moins le quart.

   2.4 L'après-midi, le dernier cours finit à trois heures et demie et je rentre à la maison.

   2.5 Ma matière préférée, c'est la géographie. C'est assez difficile, mais ce n'est jamais ennuyeux.

2.1 In the morning, I wake up at seven.   2.2 I usually arrive at school at quarter past eight.
2.3 The first lesson starts at quarter to nine.   2.4 In the afternoon, the last lesson finishes at half past three and I go home.   2.5 My favourite subject is geography. It is quite difficult, but it's never boring.

---

3. **F** You are writing to your French-speaking penfriend about a typical school day.

   Write approximately **50 words** in **French**.
   You must write something about each bullet point.

   Mention:
   - waking up
   - leaving for school
   - the beginning of the school day
   - the end of the school day
   - your favourite subject.

   3. Model answer: Je me réveille à sept heures.

   Je quitte la maison à huit heures.

   J'arrive au collège à huit heures vingt et on commence à huit heures et demie.

   On finit à trois heures et quart et je rentre à la maison.

   Ma matière préférée, c'est la physique, car c'est passionnant.

SCHOOL UNIFORM AND FACILITIES

Pour ou contre l'uniforme ?   *For or against uniform?*

1. Anaïs and her friends are talking about school uniforms.

> Avec un uniforme, c'est plus facile le matin. Pas besoin de choisir ses vêtements !
> — Anaïs

> Un uniforme à l'école ? Quelle idée bizarre ! J'ai vu l'uniforme de ma cousine anglaise, il est vraiment moche !
> — Hugo

> Avec un uniforme, tout le monde porte la même chose, alors il n'y a pas de discrimination. Par contre, c'est difficile d'être original ! Je ne sais pas.
> — Lola

> Un uniforme, c'est cher et ce n'est pas pratique. Je crois que c'est une mauvaise idée !
> — Mahmoud

What do they think of a school uniform?

Write **P** for a positive opinion, **N** for a negative opinion, and **P + N** for a positive and negative opinion.

1. Anaïs P, Hugo N, Lola P + N, Mahmoud N

Rewrite this vocabulary as two different lists; one for adjectives to be used in favour of the school uniform and another against.

bizarre	strange
cher	expensive
facile	easy
moche	ugly
pratique	practical
utile	useful

Pour (For)

Contre (Against)

Comment est ton collège ? — *What is your school like?*

Reading aloud

2. Read aloud this text, then listen to the recording to check your pronunciation.

TRACK 20

> Voici une information importante : « Je suis contre la discrimination dans la cour de récréation. Alors, l'uniforme est une bonne option. Sans hésitation ! »

> **!** In the recording, spot all the words that end in **-tion** and pay attention to the sound of that syllable: **information**, **discrimination**, **récréation**, **option**, **hésitation**. Those words don't sound like their English equivalent. Listen closely and imitate!
>
> Also check the pronunciation of the first syllable in **l'uniforme**. And at the end, pronounce **sans hésitation** as if it was one long word, with no **h** and a **z** sound in the middle.

3. Translate the paragraph above into **English**.

> 3. Here is an important piece of information: "I am against discrimination in the playground. So, uniform is a good option. Without any hesitation!"

Check you know the following nouns, to help you talk about school facilities and equipment.

le bâtiment	building	la salle d'informatique	IT room
la cour de récréation	playground	la salle de musique	music room
l'ordinateur	computer	le terrain de sport	sports ground

> **!** Remember to change **un**, **une**, **des** to **de**, or **d'**, in the negative form.
> **Il y a un grand terrain de sport.** *There is a large sports ground.*
> **Il n'y a pas de bibliothèque.** *There isn't a library.*
> **Il y a des ordinateurs.** *There are some computers.*
> **Il n'y a pas d'arbres**. *There aren't any trees.*

4. Translate these sentences into **French**.
   4.1 There are six IT rooms with computers.
   4.2 My school is in an old building. It is ugly and it is not very practical.
   4.3 We are in the town centre, so the playground is too small and there is no sports ground.
   4.4 I would like to see trees in my school. We also need music rooms. That would be great!

> *4.1 Il y a six salles d'informatique avec des ordinateurs.   4.2 Mon collège est dans un vieux bâtiment. Il est moche et ce n'est pas très pratique.   4.3 On est en centre-ville, alors la cour de récréation est trop petite et il n'y a pas de terrain de sport.   4.4 Je voudrais voir des arbres dans mon école. On a aussi besoin de salles de musique. Ce serait super !*

OPTIONS AT AGE 16

Les examens — *Exams*

Here is a reminder of the names of French school years and exams.

le collège	secondary school	le lycée	sixth form college
la sixième	Year 7	la seconde	Year 11
la cinquième	Year 8	la première	Year 12
la quatrième	Year 9	la terminale	Year 13
la troisième	Year 10	le bac / le baccalauréat	end of lycée exam
le brevet	end of collège exam	l'université	university

1. You hear Lola talking about school and exams. Choose the correct answer and write the letter.

    TRACK 21

    1.1 Lola is in the French equivalent of …
    - A Year 10.
    - B Year 11.
    - C Year 12.

    1.2 Lola will be taking an exam, called **le brevet**, …
    - A this school year.
    - B in two years' time.
    - C in three years' time.

    1.3 Lola will take an exam called **le bac** …
    - A at the end of this year.
    - B before going to university.
    - C in the first year of university.

    1.4 After school, Lola …
    - A will look for a job.
    - B will go to university.
    - C doesn't know what she will do.

    1.1 A   1.2 A   1.3 B   1.4 C

Et après ? — And then?

There are two different kinds of future tense in French.
You can use **je vais** followed by a verb in the infinitive – this is the near future tense.

| Je vais aller à l'université. | I am going to go to university. |
| Je ne vais pas avoir d'examens cette année. | I am not going to have any exams this year. |

H You can also use the future tense.

| J'irai à l'université. | I will go to university. |
| Je n'aurai pas d'examens cette année. | I won't have any exams this year. |

⭐ In the exam, using **j'espère …** (for what you hope to do), **je voudrais …** (for what you would like to do) or **j'ai l'intention de …** (for what you intend to do) will also count as using a future time frame.

❗ Turn to **page 153** for more information about the future tense.

Reading aloud

2. Read aloud this text, then listen to the recording to check your pronunciation.

TRACK 22

> Mon frère espère trouver du travail après le lycée. Moi, je ne sais pas, alors je vais peut-être faire une pause si je réussis aux examens. Par contre, ma meilleure amie a décidé : elle voudrait étudier la médecine l'année prochaine.

❗ Pay particular attention to the pronunciation of **aux examens**. The two words are pronounced as one, with a **z** sound in the middle. Same thing with **peut-être**, with a **t** sound in the middle.

3. Translate the paragraph above into **English**.

   3. My brother is hoping to find work after school. Me, I don't know, so maybe I'm going to take a break if I pass the exams. My best friend, however, has made up her mind: she would like to study medicine next year.

4. Translate these sentences into **French**.
   4.1 Are you going to go to university?
   4.2 I am hoping to find work after the exams.
   4.3 My best friend would like to study architecture.
   4.4 If I pass my exams, I am going to take a break next year.

   3.1 Tu vas aller / Tu iras à l'université ?   3.2 J'espère trouver du travail après les examens.
   3.3 Ma meilleure amie/Mon meilleur ami voudrait étudier l'architecture.   3.4 Si je réussis aux examens, je vais faire / je ferai une pause l'année prochaine.

AQA GCSE French | Theme 1

1.3

THE WORLD OF WORK

Quel métier ?   *What job?*

Check you know both the masculine and the feminine names of these jobs.

m	aide-soignant	chanteur	cuisinier	infirmier	musicien	scientifique
f	aide-soignante	chanteuse	cuisinière	infirmière	musicienne	scientifique
	nursing assistant	*singer*	*chef*	*nurse*	*musician*	*scientist*

In French, you don't need the indefinite article, **un** or **une**, to introduce the name of a job.
Je vais travailler comme médecin. *I am going to work as a doctor.*
Je rêve de devenir chanteuse. *I dream of becoming a singer.*

1. These people are talking about jobs. Which job does each person mention?
   Choose from the list and write the correct letter.
   1.1 Je voudrais être professeur.
   1.2 Je ne veux pas travailler dans un bureau.
   1.3 Mon frère rêve d'être cuisinier dans un restaurant.
   1.4 J'ai fait un stage dans un magasin de sport.
   1.5 Ma grande sœur est infirmière. Elle s'occupe d'enfants dans un hôpital.
   1.6 ❶ What extra information does person 5 mention?

A	nurse	C	office worker	E	singer	G	waitress
B	cook	D	shop assistant	F	teacher		

   1.1 F   1.2 C   1.3 B   1.4 D   1.5 A   1.6 Their sister looks after children.

2. Translate these sentences into **French**.
   2.1 I would like to work outside.
   2.2 My brother works as a nurse.
   2.3 He wants to find work in education.
   2.4 She would like to look after animals.
   2.5 They did work experience in an office.

   2.1 Je voudrais travailler dehors.   *2.2 Mon frère travaille comme infirmier.*
   2.3 Il veut trouver du travail dans l'enseignement.   *2.4 Elle voudrait s'occuper d'animaux.*
   2.5 Ils / elles ont fait un stage dans un bureau.

+	un bureau	dehors	l'enseignement	un magasin	s'occuper de	un stage
	office	*outside*	*education*	*shop*	*to look after*	*work experience*

Pourquoi ?   Why?

Here is a list of possible reasons for choosing a particular career path.

c'est bien payé	it's well paid
j'aime aider les gens	I like helping people
je voudrais être célèbre	I would like to be famous
c'est un métier passionnant	it's an exciting job
j'ai besoin de gagner de l'argent	I need to earn money

Remember that when two verbs follow each other in French, the second one is in the infinitive. The second verb comes straight after verbs like **j'aime, je veux, je voudrais**.

However, after verbs like **j'ai besoin** and **je rêve**, you need **de** or **d'** before the second verb.

Je voudrais <u>devenir</u> infirmière, car j'aime <u>aider</u> les autres.
I would like to become a nurse because I like helping others.

J'ai besoin <u>de trouver</u> un travail intéressant.
I need to find an interesting job.

Je rêve <u>d'être</u> chanteur.
I dream of being a singer.

Dictation
3. You will hear **five** sentences, repeated **three** times (the first time as a full sentence, the second time in short sections and the third time again as a full sentence).
   Write them down in **French**.

TRACK 23

3.1 Je préfère travailler dehors.   3.2 Je veux un travail passionnant et bien payé.
3.3. J'aime aider les gens, alors je vais être médecin.   3.4 Je voudrais être acteur parce que je rêve d'être célèbre.   3.5 Je vais chercher du travail, parce que j'ai besoin de gagner de l'argent.

Make sure you understand each sentence, so you can re-use them in your own speaking and writing.

Here is a translation: 3.1. *I prefer working outside.* 3.2. *I want an exciting and well-paid job.* 3.3. *I like helping people, so I want to be a doctor.* 3.4. *I would like to be an actor because I dream of being famous.* 3.5. Ⓗ *I am going to look for work because I need to earn money.*

Note that on the Foundation paper, there are only four sentences.

4. Listen to the audio and answer the **four** questions in French on future plans. Pause after each question to give your response.
   Try to answer all questions as fully as you can.

TRACK 24

4. Listen to the audio for a model response. Think about the answers you gave, and then have another go.

1.3

LOOKING FOR WORK

Tes compétences — *Your skills*

Check you know these words.

le boulot	work
le défi	challenge
en équipe	as a team
un emploi	job

1. Read this advert.

> Tu cherches un emploi ?
> Tu n'as pas peur des défis ?
> Tu aimes travailler en équipe ?
> Tu n'es pas paresseux/paresseuse ?
> Tu voudrais voyager pour ton travail ?
>
> Alors, il faut nous contacter, car nous avons besoin de tes compétences.
>
> Écris-nous à : cv@superboulot.fr

Complete these sentences. Write the letter for the correct option.

1.1 This advert is aimed at people who …
 A are looking for work. B are looking for a new course. C already have a job.

1.2 The ideal candidate must enjoy …
 A design. B challenges. C money.

1.3 They are interested in people who are …
 A good at sports. B well-dressed. C good at team work.

1.4 They are interested in people who are not …
 A serious. B lazy. C boring.

1.5 They are looking for people who can …
 A work from home. B travel for work. C speak foreign languages.

1.1 A   1.2 B   1.3 C   1.4 B   1.5 B.

L'entretien d'embauche — *The job interview*

arriver en retard	to arrive late
bien préparer l'entretien	to prepare well for the interview
expliquer ses compétences	to explain your skills
faire des recherches sur l'entreprise	to do research on the company
montrer qu'on est stressé	to show you are stressed
oublier son CV	to forget your CV
parler de son expérience	to talk about your experience
parler trop longtemps	to talk for too long
répondre à son portable pendant l'entretien	to answer your mobile during the interview
sourire	to smile

+ To learn and remember those phrases, rewrite them as two lists:
one for the things you must do: **il faut … / on doit …**
and another for the things you mustn't do: **il ne faut pas … / on ne doit pas …**

2. You hear Mahmoud talking about an interview for a job in a gym.
   Complete the sentences in **English**.

   2.1 Before the interview, Mahmoud _____.
   2.2 Mahmoud arrived _____ for the interview.
   2.3 He _____ because he was stressed.
   2.4 At the end of the interview, _____.

   2.1 did some research about the gym. 2.2 on time. 2.3 spoke too much/for too long.
   2.4 his mobile rang and he answered it.

3. Write to your French-speaking friend about an imaginary interview.
   Write approximately **90 words** in **French**.
   You must write something about each bullet point.

   Describe:
   - what you are doing to find a job
   - what went well and less well during the interview
   - what you will do differently next time.

   3. *Model answer: En ce moment, je cherche du travail parce que je voudrais gagner de l'argent. Alors, je regarde les annonces, je fais des recherches sur des entreprises intéressantes et j'envoie mon CV. Je suis allé/allée à un entretien la semaine dernière.*

   Pendant l'entretien, j'ai essayé de sourire et de montrer que je suis une personne responsable et organisée. Par contre, j'étais vraiment stressé/stressée, alors j'ai parlé beaucoup trop vite. En plus, j'ai oublié toutes mes questions. Je n'ai pas eu l'emploi.

   La prochaine fois, je vais essayer d'être plus calme !

EDUCATION AND WORK

Assemblage — *Putting it all together*

🄷 Inference questions

This style of question is found on the Higher reading paper. It is called an 'inference' question because you have to 'infer' or deduce what a word means from the context. These words are not from the defined vocabulary list so they might be new to you, but you can work them out.

Example

> Ma grand-mère avait un travail extraordinaire : elle était gardienne de phare ! Alors, elle passait son temps à regarder la mer. J'adorais aller la voir.

What is **une gardienne de phare**?

A bodyguard   **B** shepherdess   **C** lighthouse keeper

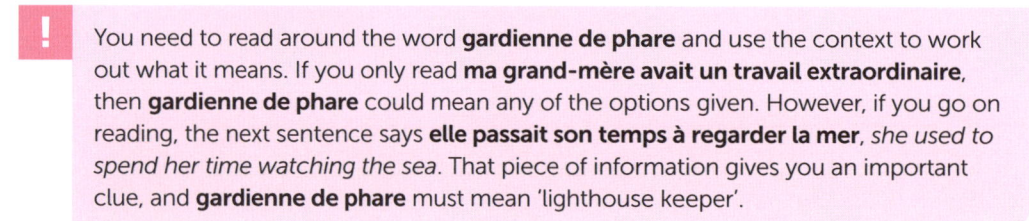

> ❗ You need to read around the word **gardienne de phare** and use the context to work out what it means. If you only read **ma grand-mère avait un travail extraordinaire**, then **gardienne de phare** could mean any of the options given. However, if you go on reading, the next sentence says **elle passait son temps à regarder la mer**, *she used to spend her time watching the sea*. That piece of information gives you an important clue, and **gardienne de phare** must mean 'lighthouse keeper'.

---

1. 🄷 Généralement, je déteste me dépêcher, je préfère prendre mon temps. Pourtant, le matin, je dois courir, sinon j'arrive en retard à l'école.

    What does **je déteste me dépêcher** mean?

    A I hate hurrying   **B** I hate going to school   **C** I hate having breakfast

2. 🄷 Le professeur dit qu'il faut utiliser un surligneur jaune ou rose pour marquer les mots de vocabulaire importants.

    What is **un surligneur**?

    A guesswork   **B** a highlighter   **C** a kind of computer

    1. A. It means 'I hate hurrying'. The writer is saying they hate hurrying. The text says that they prefer taking their time, but they'll be late for school if they don't run.
    2. B. It is a highlighter – the text talks about using it to mark important words of vocabulary.

3. You listen to Anaïs, Hugo and Lola giving Mahmoud advice before a job interview in a gym.

   Who gives each of the following pieces of advice?

   Write **A** for Anaïs, **L** for Lola, **H** for Hugo

   > ! Wait! Before listening, spend a minute thinking of one or two keywords for each item in the list. Then listen out for them. Be aware that you may not hear them all.
   >
   > For example: 3.1 à l'heure ? en retard ? 3.2 vêtements ?

   3.1 Arrive on time.
   3.2 Dress carefully.
   3.3 Mention your favourite school subject.
   3.4 Show you are enthusiastic.
   3.5 Smile.

   3.1 H 3.2 A 3.3 L 3.4 L 3.5 A

TRACK 26

Role play

4. You are talking to your French-speaking friend. Your friend will speak first. When you see this **–?–** you will have to ask a question.

   4.1 Describe your school. (Give **two** details).
   4.2 Say something your school doesn't have.
   4.3 Say what you would like to see in your school.
   4.4 Say whether you wear a uniform and what you think about it.
   ? 4.5 Ask your friend a question about their school.

   Now listen to the audio for a model response.

TRACK 27

> ⭐ In order to score full marks in the exam, you must include a verb in your response to each task.
>
> You should address your friend as **tu**.

AQA GCSE French | Theme 1

Theme 1

KEY VOCABULARY

Students are expected to know 1200 items of vocabulary for Foundation tier and a further 500 for Higher tier. This list has some of the key vocabulary for Theme 1, but there are many more words listed in the AQA specification and in an interactive spreadsheet on the AQA website.

un anniversaire	birthday
les cheveux	hair
une équipe	a team
le frère	brother
le fromage	cheese
l'informatique	IT
les légumes	vegetables
la mère	mother
le père	father
un ordinateur	computer
le poisson	fish
la sœur	sister
la viande	meat
les yeux	eyes
ennuyeux / ennuyeuse	boring
grand / grande	big
petit / petite	small
sympa	nice
plus	more
moins	less
aider	to help
s'appeler (je m'appelle…)	to be called (I am called/my name is)
arrêter	to stop
avoir peur (j'ai peur)	to be afraid (I am afraid)
boire (je bois)	to drink (I drink/I am drinking)
dormir (je dors)	to sleep (I sleep/I am sleeping)
espérer	to hope
s'entendre avec (je m'entends avec)	to get on with (I get on with)
faire (je fais)	to do, to make (I do/I am doing, I make/I am making)
manger	to eat
oublier	to forget
prendre	to take, to have
rêver	to dream
sourire	to smile
travailler	to work

Theme 1

EXAMINATION PRACTICE

People and lifestyle – Reading

Newspaper headlines

You see some headlines in a French newspaper.

A Un plus grand choix de menus végétariens dans les cantines scolaires

B Vie de famille : « Je ne m'entends pas bien avec ma demi-sœur »

C Les maladies de cœur : un défi pour les médecins

D L'uniforme scolaire de retour dans les collèges ?

E Les résultats du bac : 84,9% de réussite

Which headline matches each topic? Write the correct letter.

01 Health [1 mark]

02 Exams [1 mark]

03 Problems at home [1 mark]

Friends and family

Read this text about Kiki's friends and family.

> J'aime beaucoup mon groupe d'amis. Le weekend, on sort ou on reste à la maison pour manger une pizza et écouter de la musique. On s'amuse bien ! En plus, on discute ensemble quand il y a un devoir difficile pour le collège. Ça aide.
>
> Mes parents sont sympas et compréhensifs. Parfois, on se dispute, mais ce n'est jamais très sérieux. Mon petit frère me fait rire tous les jours, car il est vraiment très drôle. En conclusion, je ne peux pas imaginer la vie sans ma famille ou sans mes amis. Ils sont tous importants pour moi !
>
> **Kiki**

Answer the following questions in **English**.

04 What do Kiki and her friends do at the weekend at home? Give **two** details. [2 marks]

05 What happens when they have difficult homework for school? [1 mark]

06 What does Kiki say about her arguments with her parents? [1 mark]

07 Give **one** detail about the younger member of the family. [1 mark]

08 Who is more important in Kiki's life? Friends or family or both? [1 mark]

AQA GCSE French

People and lifestyle – Listening

You hear an online item about mental health. The presenter lists some reasons why young people are stressed. Which **four** things are mentioned? Write the correct letters.

TRACK 28

A	Illnesses
B	Life at home
C	Unhealthy eating
D	Bad sleep patterns
E	School life and exams
F	Relationships with friends

Part 1

01 Reason 1 _____ [1 mark]

02 Reason 2 _____ [1 mark]

Part 2

03 Reason 3 _____ [1 mark]

04 Reason 4 _____ [1 mark]

You hear Nathan telling his aunt what lessons he has at school today.
Complete the sentences in **English**.

TRACK 29

05 Today is an easy day because it is … [1 mark]

06 Nathan's last lesson finishes at … [1 mark]

07 Nathan's favourite subject is … [1 mark]

08 His physics lesson starts at … [1 mark]

🅗 Dictation

09 You will now hear **five** short sentences.

Listen carefully and, using your knowledge of French sounds, write down in **French** exactly what you hear for each sentence.

TRACK 30

You will hear each sentence **three** times: the first time as a full sentence, the second time in short sections and the third time again as a full sentence.

Use your knowledge of French sounds and grammar to make sure that what you have written makes sense. Check carefully that your spelling is accurate.

(Note that, on the Foundation paper, there are only **four** sentences.) [10 marks]

People and lifestyle – Speaking

Role play

You are speaking to your Swiss friend. Your friend will speak first.

Listen to the audio, pause after each question and answer in **French**.

You should address your friend as **tu**.

When you see this **– ? –** you will have to ask a question.

In order to score full marks, you must include at least **one** verb in your response to each task.

    01 Say whether you like sports and why/why not. (Give **one** opinion and **one** reason.)

    02 Say what you usually do to stay healthy. (Give **two** details.)

    03 Say at what time you went to bed last night. (Give **one** detail.)

    04 Say what you had for breakfast this morning. (Give **two** details.)

?   05 Ask your friend a question about healthy living.   [10 marks]

TRACK 31

Photo card

06 Look at the two photos and make notes about what you can say about them.
Then set a timer and talk about the content of the photos.   [5 marks]

    F Foundation students have **one minute** to talk, and **H** Higher students have **a minute and a half**.

TRACK 32

Photo 1

Photo 2

07 Now answer the recorded questions for the unprepared conversation on the theme.   [20 marks]

TRACK 33

> After you have spoken about the content of the photos, you will be asked questions related to any of the topics within the theme of People and lifestyle. Listen to the recording. Pause after you hear each question and try to answer them in as much detail as possible.
>
> Then listen to the questions again, with model responses. Go back and have another go yourself at answering the questions.

AQA GCSE French

People and lifestyle – Writing

F Using your knowledge of grammar, complete the following sentences in **French**.
Choose the correct French word from the three options available. [5 marks]

Example:

Le cours d'histoire ____*finit*____ à onze heures.

fini   finis   finit

01 Mon chat a les yeux _____

vert   verte   verts

02 Je vais _____ à l'université.

allé   aller   allez

03 Je joue _____ basket le samedi.

au   aux   du

04 Je pense que c'est une _____ idée.

bon   bonne   bons

05 J'_____ bien ma prof de géographie.

aime   aimer   aimes

06 **F** + **H** Translate the following sentences into **French**. [10 marks]
- I went to school yesterday.
- I would like to go to university.
- In my opinion, history is never boring.
- She eats fruit every day, but she hates apples.
- He gets on well with his sister and his parents.

07 **H** Write a short piece about healthy living for your school newsletter.

Write approximately **150 words** in **French**. You must write something about each bullet point.

Describe:
- what you have to do and not do in order to be healthy.
- what you have learned from the past and will try to do in the future. [25 marks]

TOPICS FOR THEME 2
Popular culture

Specification coverage

Topic 1   Free-time activities
Topic 2   Customs, festivals and celebrations
Topic 3   Celebrity culture

Information about the four papers for Foundation (F) and Higher (H) tiers:

Paper 1 – Listening

Written exam:
35 minutes (F), 45 minutes (H)
40 marks (F), 50 marks (H)
25% of GCSE

The recording is controlled by the invigilator with built-in repetitions and pauses.

Each exam includes 5 minutes' reading time at the start of the question paper before the listening material is played and 2 minutes at the end of the recording to check your work.

Section A – Listening comprehension questions in English, to be answered in English or non-verbally ((F) 32 marks, (H) 40 marks).

Section B – Dictation where students transcribe 4 sentences ((F) 8 marks) or 5 sentences ((H) 10 marks).

Paper 2 – Speaking

Non-exam assessment (NEA):
7–9 minutes (F) or 10–12 minutes (H) +
15 minutes' supervised preparation time
50 marks, 25% of GCSE

Role play – 10 marks, 1–1.5 minutes. (F) (H)

Reading aloud passage and short conversation – 15 marks.
Recommended time 2–2.5 minutes (F) and 3–3.5 minutes (H).
Minimum 35 words (F) and minimum 50 words (H).

Photo card discussion (two photos) – 25 marks.
Photo card discussion time:
4–5 minutes (F) and 6–7 minutes (H).

Paper 3 – Reading

Written exam: 45 minutes (F), 1 hour (H)
50 marks, 25% of GCSE

Section A – Reading comprehension questions in English, to be answered in English or non-verbally (40 marks).

Section B – Translation from French into English, minimum of 35 words (F) or 50 words (H) (10 marks).

Paper 4 – Writing

Written exam: 1 hour 10 minutes (F),
1 hour 15 minutes (H)
50 marks, 25% of GCSE

Set of three short writing tasks. (F) only.
25 marks.

Translation of sentences from English into French, minimum 35 words (F), or 50 words (H) (10 marks).

Produce a piece of writing in response to three compulsory bullet points, approximately 90 words in total. Choose from two questions (15 marks). (F) (H)

Open-ended writing task.
Two compulsory bullet points, approximately 150 words in total. Choose from two questions. (25 marks). (H) only.

2.1

ACTIVITIES AT HOME

Mon temps libre   *My free time*

1. Anaïs and her friends are saying what they do to relax at home.

> *Pour me relaxer, j'adore faire des gâteaux avec mon petit frère. Après, on les mange en famille. Et on boit du thé !*
> — Anaïs

> *Moi, pour oublier les problèmes et les disputes, je vais dans ma chambre et je ne parle à personne. Je préfère lire un roman.*
> — Hugo

> *J'aime regarder des vidéos amusantes avec mes copains. On rit bien ensemble ! Ou alors, je joue avec Tommy, mon petit chien. C'est super pour se relaxer.*
> — Lola

> *Moi, ce qui me relaxe, c'est d'écouter de la musique ou de jouer de la guitare.*
> — Mahmoud

Who does what to relax? Write **A** for Anaïs, **H** for Hugo, **L** for Lola, and **M** for Mahmoud.

1.1 Gets into a book.
1.2 Has fun with friends.
1.3 Plays an instrument.
1.4 Plays with their dog.
1.5 Spends time with the family.
1.6 Wants to be left alone.

1.1 H   1.2 L   1.3 M   1.4 L   1.5 A   1.6 H

écouter de la musique	to listen to music
faire des gâteaux	to bake cakes
faire la cuisine	to cook
jouer	to play
lire des romans	to read novels
regarder des vidéos	to watch videos
rire	laugh

! Remember: **jouer au / à la / à l' / aux** + game,
jouer du / de la / de l' / des + musical instrument.
Je joue aux jeux vidéo. *I play video games.*
Il joue du piano. *He plays the piano.*

À mon avis — *In my opinion*

Make sure you vary the ways of presenting your opinion.

Je trouve ça nul.	I think it's rubbish.
Je ne trouve pas ça intéressant.	I don't find that interesting.
Pour moi, c'est essentiel.	For me, it's essential.
À mon avis, c'est ennuyeux.	In my opinion, it's boring.
Je pense que c'est fascinant.	I think it's fascinating.
Je crois que c'est complètement stupide.	I think it's completely stupid.

+ To help you learn and remember the opening phrases, write two lists: one of positive and the other of negative opinions.

! Whatever you are talking about, the adjective that comes after **c'est** is always masculine singular. E.g: **C'est énervant.** *It's annoying.*

2. Translate these sentences into **French**.
   - 2.1 Music is essential for me.
   - 2.2 I never watch television with my parents.
   - 2.3 I don't like playing cards because I hate losing.
   - 2.4 I find reality TV stupid and I prefer watching comedies.
   - 2.5 In my opinion, documentaries about animals are fascinating.

   2.1 La musique est essentielle pour moi.
   2.2 Je ne regarde jamais la télévision avec mes parents.
   2.3 Je n'aime pas jouer aux cartes parce que je déteste perdre.
   2.4 Je trouve la téléréalité stupide et je préfère regarder des comédies.
   2.5 À mon avis, les documentaires sur les animaux sont passionnants.

! Note: If you have a second verb after something like **j'aime**, **je déteste** or **je préfère**, leave it in the infinitive form. **J'aime chanter.** *I like singing.* See **page 148** for infinitives.

Role play

3. Plan what you are going to say in this role play. Then play the recording and pause after you hear each question or statement, so you can give your response. When you see this **–?–** you will have to ask a question.

   You are talking to your French-speaking friend about free time.
   Your friend will speak first.

   - 3.1 Say what you do to relax at home. (Give **two** details).
   - 3.2 Say what you never watch on television and why.
   - 3.3 Say whether you prefer listening to music alone or with friends and why.
   - **?** 3.4 Ask your friend a question about music.
   - 3.5 Say what kind of games you like playing and why.

TRACK 34

2.1

OUTDOOR ACTIVITIES

Sortir — *Going out*

Here are some ideas for going out.

aller à un concert	to go to a concert
bien s'amuser	to have a good time
faire des randonnées à la campagne	to go hiking in the countryside
faire du skate	to go skateboarding
faire les magasins	to go shopping
prendre (un ballon)	to take (a ball)
profiter du beau temps	to enjoy the good weather
promener le chien	to walk the dog

+ Rewrite this vocabulary list in a different order: start with what you like best and end with what you like least.

---

1. You hear Mahmoud talking about free time with his family.

   Select the correct answer to each question.

   TRACK 35

   1.1 Last weekend, Mahmoud …
   - A went to a great concert with his family.
   - B enjoyed going to a concert with his friends.
   - C stayed at home because he couldn't afford to go to a concert.

   1.2 Mahmoud usually spends his free time …
   - A with his dad.
   - B with his friends.
   - C with his family or his friends.

   1.3 Mahmoud often goes on …
   - A great country walks with his family.
   - B boring country walks with his family.
   - C lovely camping trips in the forest with his friends.

   1.4 What Mahmoud doesn't like is …
   - A going shopping.
   - B buying clothes online.
   - C going to the cinema with his dad.

   1.1 B   1.2 C   1.3 A   1.4 A

52 ClearRevise

Être ensemble — *Being together*

2. Translate these sentences into **English**.

   2.1 Il sourit quand il est content.
   2.2 On pense qu'il faut profiter du beau temps.
   2.3 J'aime sortir promener le chien tous les matins.
   2.4 Je déteste les sports dangereux. Je préfère les randonnées en forêt.
   2.5 Je prends toujours un ballon quand je vais au parc avec mes copains.

   2.1 He smiles when he is happy.
   2.2 We think we/you have to make the most of the good weather.
   2.3 I like going out to walk the dog every morning.
   2.4 I hate dangerous sports. I prefer walks in the forest.
   2.5 I always take a ball when I go out with my friends.

3. **F** You and your French friends are sharing photos on Snapchat. What's in this photo? Write **five** sentences in **French**.

   Model response:
   3.1 Sur la photo, je suis avec mes copains.
   3.2 On est au parc.
   3.3 Il y a Alicia avec le ballon, Théo et moi avec le skate.
   3.4 On aime être ensemble.
   3.5 On est contents et on sourit !

2.1

TV AND CINEMA

C'était comment ? — *What was it like?*

Here are some adjectives and adverbs you can use to describe how you feel about something.

Adjectives	
émouvant	*moving*
extraordinaire	*extraordinary*
génial	*great, cool*
mauvais	*bad*
nul	*rubbish*
triste	*sad*

Adverbs	
absolument	*absolutely*
assez	*quite*
particulièrement	*particularly*
trop	*too*
un peu	*a little*
vraiment	*really*

To say how you felt about an event, start with a verb, such as **c'était** or **j'ai trouvé**.

<u>C'était</u> émouvant. *It was moving.*
<u>J'ai trouvé</u> ça triste. *I found that sad.*

To express your opinion more accurately, you could add an adverb before the adjective.

C'était <u>vraiment</u> fantastique. *It was really moving.*
J'ai trouvé ça <u>trop</u> triste. *I found that too sad.*

! Whatever you are talking about, the adjective that comes after **c'était** is always masculine singular. E.g: **C'était mauvais.** *It was bad.*

And here is a list of types of films and TV programmes.

la comédie	*comedy*
les dessins animés	*cartoons*
le documentaire	*documentary*
le film d'action	*action film*
le film d'horreur	*horror film*
la téléréalité	*reality TV*

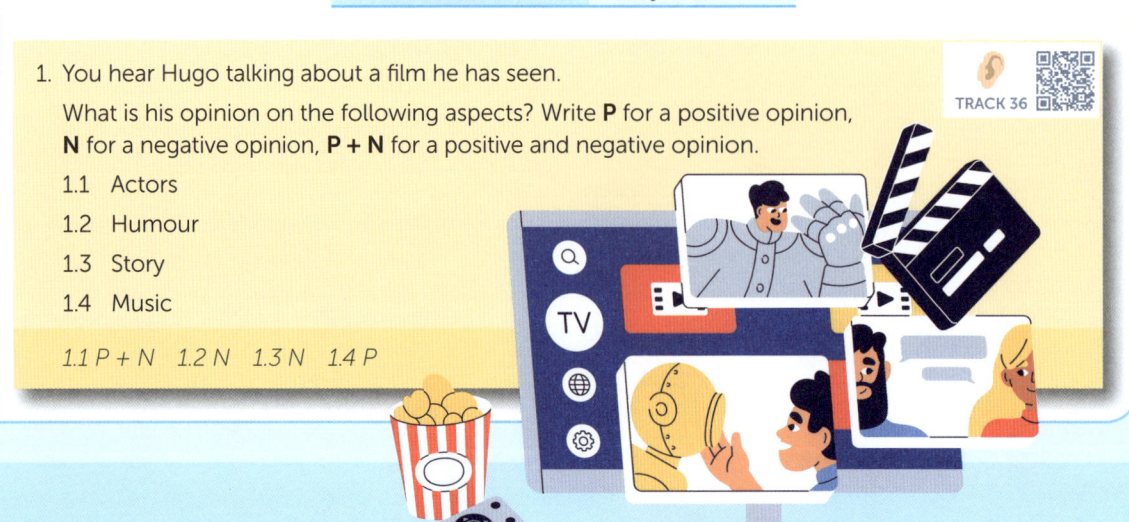

---

1. You hear Hugo talking about a film he has seen.

   What is his opinion on the following aspects? Write **P** for a positive opinion, **N** for a negative opinion, **P + N** for a positive and negative opinion.

   1.1 Actors
   1.2 Humour
   1.3 Story
   1.4 Music

   1.1 P + N   1.2 N   1.3 N   1.4 P

   TRACK 36

Un bon film — *A good film*

When talking about the past, you need to choose between the perfect and the imperfect tense.

Use the perfect tense to describe what you, or someone else, did.
On a regardé un film. *We watched a film.*
Je suis allé au cinéma. *I went to the cinema.*

Use the imperfect tense to describe how things were or what was going on.
Il y avait trois chiens. *There were three dogs.*
Je regardais une comédie. *I was watching a comedy.*

Also, use the imperfect tense to talk about something that used to happen regularly.
On jouait au foot tous les jours. *We used to play football every day.*

Reading aloud
2. Read aloud this text, then listen to the recording to check your pronunciation.

TRACK 37

> Je suis allé au cinéma et j'ai vu un film super. C'était l'histoire de trois jeunes chanteurs pendant les années soixante-dix. Les acteurs jouaient vraiment bien et la musique était absolument fantastique. J'ai trouvé ça passionnant.

! Note: The **-ent** of **jouaient** is silent (as with all **ils/elles** forms of verbs). On the other hand, do pronounce the **-ment** ending of the adverbs **vraiment** and **absolument**.

3. Translate the paragraph above into **English**.

> 3. *I went to the cinema, and I saw a great film. It was the story of three young singers during the seventies. The actors played really well and the music was absolutely fantastic. I found it fascinating.*

The past participle of **-er** verbs ends in **-é**. The past participles of other verbs are less regular and don't follow a predictable pattern. Start by learning the following ones.

Infinitive	Past participle	English (I have...)
boire	bu	*drunk*
entendre	entendu	*heard*
faire	fait	*done*
prendre, comprendre, apprendre	pris, compris, appris	*taken, understood, learned*
rire	ri	*laughed*
voir	vu	*seen*

2.1 MAKING PLANS

Mon temps libre — *My free time*

1. Read about Anaïs's plans for next weekend.

   Le week-end prochain, je vais faire un gâteau pour l'anniversaire de mon petit frère. Il va ouvrir son cadeau dimanche matin et je crois qu'il va être très content. C'est un nouveau vélo ! L'après-midi, on va probablement aller au parc avec le vélo. Lola et son chien Tommy vont peut-être venir avec nous. On va bien s'amuser ! J'espère qu'il va faire beau.

   Answer the following questions in **English**.
   1.1 Why is Anaïs going to make a cake?
   1.2 Why does she think her brother will be happy?

   Complete these sentences. Select the correct letter.
   1.3 On Sunday afternoon, they will probably...
      A forget about the bike.
      B take Lola's dog for a walk.
      C go to the park with the new bike.
   1.4 Anaïs is hoping for...
      A a happy dog.
      B good weather.
      C a beautiful bike.

   1.1 Because it's her brother's birthday.   1.2 Because he'll be getting a new bike.   1.3 C.   1.4 B

demain	tomorrow
après-demain	the day after tomorrow
le week-end prochain	next weekend
la semaine prochaine	next week
le mois prochain	next month
l'année prochaine	next year

Prochain goes with masculine nouns, and rhymes with **demain**.
Prochaine goes with feminine nouns, and rhymes with **semaine**.

Qu'est-ce que tu vas faire ? — *What are you going to do?*

Let's compare the two future tenses. Check out what's in the left and right column of this table.

Near future tense	Simple future tense ⓗ
Je vais avoir un vélo. *I am going to have a bike.*	J'aurai un vélo. *I'll have a bike.*
Tu vas être content. *You're going to be pleased.*	Tu seras content. *You'll be pleased.*
Il va faire beau temps. *The weather is going to be good.*	Il fera beau temps. *The weather will be good.*
On va aller au parc. *We are going to go to the park.*	On ira au parc. *We'll go to the park.*

! Note that, for the ⓕ Foundation paper, you only need to know the near future (the left column).
Turn to **page 153** for more details about these two future tenses.

Dictation

2. You will hear **five** sentences, repeated **three** times (the first time as a full sentence, the second time in short sections and the third time again as a full sentence).
Write them down in **French**.

    2.1 Elle va aller au cinéma.   2.2 On va jouer aux cartes.   2.3 Tu vas faire les magasins ?
    2.4 Je ne vais pas sortir ce soir.   2.5 Je ferai mes devoirs demain.

! Note that on the ⓕ Foundation paper, there are only **four** sentences.

+ Make sure you understand each sentence, so you can re-use them in your own speaking and writing. Here is a translation: 2.1 *She is going to go to the cinema.*   2.2 *We are going to play cards.*   2.3 *Are you going to go shopping?*   2.4 *I am not going to go out tonight.*   2.5 *I will do my homework tomorrow.*

3. Translate these sentences into **French**.
    3.1 You are going to laugh! (use **tu**)
    3.2 She is going to hate the music.
    3.3 The weather is going to be cold next week.
    3.4 I am going to open my presents this evening.
    3.5 They are going to make a chocolate cake for my birthday.

    3.1 Tu vas rire !   3.2 Elle va détester la musique.   3.3 Il va faire froid la semaine prochaine.
    3.4 Je vais ouvrir mes cadeaux ce soir.   3.5 Ils/Elles vont faire un gâteau au chocolat pour mon anniversaire.

2.1

PAST, PRESENT AND FUTURE

Hier, aujourd'hui et demain   *Yesterday, today and tomorrow*

1. Lola is talking about her free-time activities, past, present and future.

> Avant, j'aimais regarder la télé et j'allais au cinéma avec ma mère et ma copine Anaïs. On a vu beaucoup de films comiques ensemble.
>
> Maintenant que j'ai mon petit chien Tommy, je préfère aller au parc. Mes copains viennent avec moi et on joue au foot ensemble. Quand Tommy est avec nous, il court vite après le ballon. Ça nous fait rire !
>
> Pendant les prochaines vacances, je vais faire un stage de pâtisserie. Je vais apprendre à faire des gâteaux et je vais essayer d'être aussi bonne qu'Anaïs !

Write **P** for something Lola did in the past, **N** for an activity she does now, and **F** for an activity she wants to do in the future.

1.1 Baking
1.2 Cinema
1.3 Football
1.4 Television

1.1 Baking F   1.2 Cinema P   1.3 Football N   1.4 Television P

---

hier	*yesterday*
avant-hier	*the day before yesterday*
le week-end dernier	*last weekend*
la semaine dernière	*last week*
le mois dernier	*last month*
l'année dernière	*last year*

Dernier goes with masculine nouns, and you don't hear the final **r**.
Dernière goes with feminine nouns, and rhymes with **hier**. You hear the final **r**.

aujourd'hui	*today*
d'habitude	*usually*
en ce moment	*at the moment*
généralement	*generally*
maintenant	*now*

Avant — *Before*

2. **F** Using your knowledge of grammar, complete the following sentences in **French**. Choose the correct French word from the three options in the grid.
This type of exercise appears in the Foundation writing exam **only**.

Example: J'ai ___gagné___ le match à dix heures.
   gagne   gagné   gagner

2.1 Hier matin, j'ai _____ le chien.
   promenais   promène   promené

2.2 Le week-end dernier, je _____ au cinéma.
   allait   est allé   suis allé

2.3 Avant, je _____ de la natation une fois par semaine.
   faire   faisais   fait

2.4 C'_____ l'histoire d'une championne de tennis belge.
   ai   était   été

2.5 J'ai _____ beaucoup de films d'action avec mon frère.
   voir   vois   vu

2.1 promené   2.2 suis allé   2.3 faisais   2.4 était   2.5 vu

---

Knowing your verbs well will help you complete this type of exercise without much problem.

For example, in 1.1, you already have **j'ai** (part of **avoir**, auxiliary verb). This means the next word must be a past participle. In the case of an **-er** verb, the past participle ends in **-é**. Then in 2.2, the use of **je** gives you the clue that the next word will start with a consonant not a vowel.

Role play

3. Plan what you are going to say in this role play. Then play the recording and pause after you hear each question or statement, so you can give your response.
When you see this **–?–** you will have to ask a question.

TRACK 39

You are talking to your French-speaking friend. Your friend will speak first.

3.1 Say what you did to relax last weekend. (Give **two** details.)
3.2 Describe a film you have seen recently.
3.3 Say what you used to watch on TV when you were younger.
3.4 Say what you are going to do next weekend. (Give **two** details.)
? 3.5 Ask your friend a question about television.

! In order to score full marks in the exam, you **must** include a verb in your response to each task. When you ask a question, address your friend as **tu** not **vous**.

AQA GCSE French | Theme 2

2.1

FREE-TIME ACTIVITIES

Assemblage — *Putting it all together*

1. You hear the first part of a podcast about activities teenagers would enjoy doing with their family.

   Which **four** activities are suggested? Write the correct letters.

   TRACK 40

A	Cooking
B	Going to the cinema
C	Laughing
D	Making videos
E	Playing cards
F	Playing games in the forest

   E, A, B, F.

> **!** For this type of listening task, beware of distractors which may lead you to the wrong answer.
>
> For example, if you heard **on rit beaucoup**, *we laugh a lot*, in the first activity suggestion, you may have thought that laughing was the right answer. That was, however, only a side comment about the fact that you can have a good laugh while playing cards.

2. You hear the final part of the podcast about teenagers and family life.

   Answer the questions in **English**.

   TRACK 41

   2.1 What is essential in family life?

   2.2 What are the **two** suggestions given to achieve that?

   2.1 laughing   2.2 sharing jokes, watching comedy videos

> **+** Always try to hook your response on more than one word. For example, if you were not sure whether you really heard **rire** (*to laugh*), the next part with **drôle** and **comiques** could help you confirm it.
>
> Once you have done both of the listening tasks on this page, listen again while following the transcript that is available online. Make a list of key phrases you want to learn and re-use.

3. You are writing to your French-speaking penfriend about a film you have seen.

   Write approximately **90 words** in **French**.
   You must write something about each bullet point.

   Describe:
   - what films you normally like and why
   - a film you have seen recently
   - the next film you are planning to see.

   3. *Example of a response: Je vais souvent au cinéma avec mes copains. En général, je préfère les films drôles, parce que j'aime rire.*
   Récemment, on a vu un film canadien très émouvant. C'était l'histoire de deux stylistes qui dessinent des uniformes scolaires. Ce n'était pas un film comique, mais j'ai trouvé l'histoire particulièrement originale. En plus, les acteurs jouaient vraiment bien. Par contre, j'ai détesté la musique, car elle était trop bizarre à mon avis.
   Samedi prochain, ma cousine voudrait aller au cinéma avec moi. Je ne sais pas encore quel film on va choisir.

   ⭐ This student has covered all the bullet points, and used a variety of tenses, including the perfect and the imperfect. They have used a variety of ways to express their opinions, such as **j'ai trouvé** or **à mon avis**. They have also made good use of adverbs such as **très**, **particulièrement**, **assez**, or **trop** to give more meaning to the adjectives.

4. **Ⓗ** You are writing an article about your favourite free-time activities for a social media post.

   Write approximately **150 words** in **French**.
   You must write something about each bullet point.

   Mention:
   - what you enjoy doing with your family and describe something you did recently
   - what you prefer doing with friends and say what you are planning to do soon.

   4. *Example of a response: J'aime passer du temps avec ma famille. On rit beaucoup ensemble. On se dispute de temps en temps, mais généralement on s'entend bien. La semaine dernière, c'était l'anniversaire de ma petite sœur. Alors, on a mangé un gâteau au chocolat délicieux et on est sortis faire une promenade en forêt avec le chien. C'était vraiment sympa et ma petite sœur était très contente.*

   D'habitude, le week-end, je sors avec mes amis. On s'amuse bien ensemble. On joue au foot et au basket. Près de chez moi, il y a un parc où on peut faire du skate. Quand il pleut, on aime bien rester à la maison pour manger une pizza, écouter de la musique ou regarder des vidéos amusantes. Le week-end prochain, on va aller au concert de notre chanteur préféré. Je pense que ça va être extraordinaire ! Je voudrais faire ça plus souvent, mais c'est difficile à cause du prix des billets.

   ⭐ This student has written a separate paragraph for each bullet point. They have used a range of verbs, including reflexives and different tenses: present, perfect, imperfect, as well as the near future (**aller** + infinitive) and **je voudrais** + infinitive to say what the they would like to do.

2.2

CELEBRATIONS

Faire la fête   *Partying*

1. Mahmoud is describing birthday celebrations in his family.

> Dans ma famille, on aime célébrer les anniversaires. On partage un gâteau et on reçoit des cadeaux. (J'adore recevoir des cadeaux !) En général, on fait quelque chose de spécial : on invite quelques amis à la maison ou on va à un spectacle ou à un concert.
>
> La semaine dernière, c'était l'anniversaire de mon père. On a fait une grande fête de famille à la maison. Mon père a chanté des chansons et tout le monde a dansé. C'était génial !

Answer the following questions in **English**.

1.1 How do they celebrate birthdays in Mahmoud's family?
1.2 Give **two** examples of special things they do for birthdays.
1.3 When was his father's birthday?
1.4 Where did they celebrate and how?

1.1 They share a cake and receive presents.
1.2 They invite friends to their house, or go to a show or a concert.   *1.3 last week.*
1.4 They had a big family party at home. His father sang and everyone danced.

Make sure you know these key words relating to celebrations.

le cadeau	gift, present
la chanson	song
la fête	party
le gâteau	cake
partager	to share
recevoir	to receive
le repas	meal
le spectacle	show

! Remember, for French words ending in **-au**, add an **-x** in the plural.
le cadeau, *present*   **les cadeaux**, *presents*
le gâteau, *cake*   **les gâteaux**, *cakes*

Also learn the main irregular forms of **recevoir**: **je reçois**, *I receive*   **j'ai reçu**, *I received*

Bon anniversaire ! *Happy birthday!*

There are two ways to say 'we' in French: **nous** and **on**.
Nous is more formal, **on** is much more commonly used.
Make sure you use the correct verb endings for each of them.

on <u>mange</u> un gâteau	nous <u>mangeons</u> un gâteau	*we eat a cake*
on <u>fait</u> la fête	nous <u>faisons</u> la fête	*we party*
on <u>a</u> dansé	nous <u>avons</u> dansé	*we danced*
on <u>est</u> allés à une fête	nous <u>sommes</u> allés à une fête	*we went to a party*
on <u>va</u> avoir des cadeaux	nous <u>allons</u> avoir des cadeaux	*we are going to get presents*

! Apart from **nous sommes** (*we are*, from **être**), the **nous** form of a verb always ends in **-ons**.

2. Translate into **French**.

   Use either **on** or **nous** for 'we', as you prefer – both are correct! But you must use the right form of the verb to match it.

   2.1 We usually eat a special meal at home.
   2.2 We had a party for my birthday last weekend.
   2.3 We went to a show to celebrate my sister's birthday.
   2.4 We all like to share a birthday cake and receive presents.
   2.5 We are going to celebrate my mother's birthday next week.

   2.1 D'habitude, on mange/nous mangeons un repas spécial à la maison.
   2.2 On a fait/Nous avons fait une fête pour mon anniversaire le week-end dernier.
   2.3 On est allés/Nous sommes allés à un spectacle pour fêter/célébrer l'anniversaire de ma sœur.
   2.4 On aime/Nous aimons tous partager un gâteau et recevoir des cadeaux.
   2.5 On va/Nous allons célébrer/fêter l'anniversaire de ma mère la semaine prochaine.

Role play

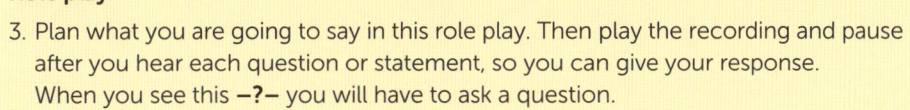

3. Plan what you are going to say in this role play. Then play the recording and pause after you hear each question or statement, so you can give your response.
   When you see this **–?–** you will have to ask a question.

   You are talking to your French-speaking friend about birthdays.
   Your friend will speak first.

   3.1 Say what you normally do for your birthday. (Give **two** details.)
   ? 3.2 Ask your friend one question about birthdays.
   3.3 Say what you did recently to celebrate the birthday of someone you are close to.
   3.4 Say what you think about receiving presents or money. (Give **one** opinion and **one** reason.)
   3.5 Say how you will celebrate your next birthday. (Give **one** detail.)

2.2

FESTIVALS AROUND THE WORLD

Divali, la fête des lumières — Diwali, the festival of lights

Listen out for the following words and phrases in the task below.

une fête religieuse	a religious festival
une fête hindoue	a Hindu festival
un jour férié	a bank holiday
un vêtement traditionnel	an item of traditional clothing
un voisin	a neighbour

1. You hear Hugo and Anaïs talking about Diwali in Mauritius.

    TRACK 43

    Complete the sentences in **English**.

    1.1 The festival of lights is in …
    1.2 It is a Hindu festival, but in Mauritius it is also a …
    1.3 On that day, many Mauritians wear …
    1.4 People decorate their houses and gardens with …
    1.5 They go to their friends and neighbours and take …

    1.1 November   1.2 national/bank holiday   1.3 traditional clothes   1.4 lights   1.5 small cakes.

Here are some words to refer to a person's religion.

bouddhiste	Buddhist
chrétien / chrétienne	Christian
hindou / hindoue	Hindu
juif / juive	Jewish
musulman / musulmane	Muslim

Note the absence of articles in French in the following sentences.
The French adjective (**musulman**, **bouddhiste**, etc.) also doesn't have a capital letter.

Je suis musulman. *I am a Muslim.*   **Elle est bouddhiste.** *She is a Buddhist.*

And here are some words to refer to places of worship.

une église	church
une mosquée	mosque
une synagogue	synagogue
un temple	temple

Les jours fériés — Bank holidays

2. Translate these sentences into **English**.

    2.1 En France, le 14 juillet est un jour férié.
    2.2 La fête nationale au Québec, c'est le 24 juin.
    2.3 Les musulmans célèbrent la fin du Ramadan.
    2.4 Les gens décorent leurs maisons avec des lumières.
    2.5 Nous avons préparé des petits gâteaux pour nos voisins.

2.1 In France, the 14th of July is a bank holiday.   2.2 The national holiday in Québec is on the 24th of June.   2.3 Muslim people celebrate the end of Ramadan.   2.4 People decorate their houses with lights.   2.5 We have made/prepared small/little cakes for our neighbours.

3. Translate into **French**.

    3.1 I like bank holidays!
    3.2 We decorated the garden with lights.
    3.3 The neighbours came to share cakes with us.
    3.4 Everyone wanted to dance and have a good time.
    3.5 Next weekend I am going to watch the fireworks with my friends.

> **le feu d'artifice** = *fireworks*

3.1 J'aimes les jours fériés !   3.2 On a décoré/Nous avons décoré le jardin avec des lumières.   3.3 Les voisins sont venus partager des gâteaux avec nous.   3.4 Tout le monde voulait danser et s'amuser.   3.5 Le week-end prochain, je vais regarder le feu d'artifice avec mes amis.

+ When checking your translation, ask yourself the following questions:

Have I spelt this plural correctly? Have I put the second verb in the infinitive? Have I checked the word order of each sentence? Have I got the right past tense? Is this perfect tense verb conjugated with **avoir** or **être**?

Reading aloud

4. Read aloud the following text, then listen to the recording to check your pronunciation.

> E<u>n</u> Fra<u>n</u>ce, on ma<u>n</u>ge, on da<u>n</u>se et on cha<u>n</u>te qua<u>n</u>d on fait la fête.
> Et souv<u>en</u>t, les g<u>en</u>s da<u>n</u>sent da<u>n</u>s la rue. C'est vraim<u>en</u>t marra<u>n</u>t !

TRACK 44

+ Listen out for the nasal **-an** / **-en** sounds, underlined. These two spellings sound exactly the same. Listen and imitate the sound in these words. Note that the final **-ent** of **dansent** is silent.

2.2

SPECIAL DAYS

La fête de la musique   *World Music Day*

1. Translate these sentences into **English**.
   1.1 Tout le monde peut participer.
   1.2 Tous les concerts sont gratuits.
   1.3 Le 21 juin, c'est le premier jour de l'été.
   1.4 Cette fête se passe tous les ans depuis 1982.

   1.1 Everybody can take part.   1.2 All concerts are free.   1.3 The 21st of June is the first day of summer.   1.4 This festival / special day has been taking place every year since 1982.

> **!** You will hear most of those sentences in the listening task that follows. Listen out for them.

2. You hear Lola and Mahmoud talking about a popular day in France: **la fête de la musique**.

   TRACK 45

   Select the correct answer to each question.

   2.1 World Music Day takes place …
       A every year on the 4th of July.
       B every year on the 21st of June.
       C every other year on the 22nd of June.

   2.2 On that day, all concerts are …
       A free.   **B** in private gardens.   **C** happening in big cities.

   2.3 World Music Day was created in …
       A 1922   **B** 1942   **C** 1982

   2.4 What's special is that …
       A anybody can take part.
       B only fabulous musicians can take part.
       C professional musicians cannot take part.

   2.1 B   2.2 A   2.3 C   2.4 A

There are four different forms of the word for 'all' in French (translated as *all*, *whole* or *every*, depending on the context).

masculine singular	tout	tout le monde	*everyone*
feminine singular	toute	toute ma famille	*my whole family*
masculine plural	tous	tous les concerts	*all the concerts*
feminine plural	toutes	toutes les fêtes	*all the festivals*

Depuis — *For / Since*

Use the present tense with **depuis** to say how long or since when something has been happening.

| Je joue de la guitare depuis deux ans. | I have been playing the guitar for two years. |
| On est à la fête de la musique depuis midi. | We have been at the music festival since midday. |

3. Translate into **French**.
   3.1 I have been listening to music since this morning.
   3.2 World Music Day has been happening in France since 1982.
   3.3 He has been playing the saxophone since the age of twelve.
   3.4 I think the musicians have been playing outside for two hours.
   3.5 On the 21st of June all concerts are free and everybody can take part.

   3.1 J'écoute de la musique depuis ce matin.   3.2 La fête de la musique a lieu en France depuis 1982.   3.3 Il joue du saxophone depuis l'âge de 12 ans.   3.4 Je crois que les musiciens jouent dehors depuis deux heures.   3.5 Le 21 juin, tous les concerts sont gratuits et tout le monde peut participer.

Photo card

4. Look at the photo and make notes about it. Then set a timer and talk about it for about **45 seconds**. At the end, listen to the recording for a model answer.

   TRACK 46

+ To prepare for that task, have another look at all the language in this spread and adapt it.

   In the exam you have to say something about two photos, and you have to talk for **one minute** (Foundation) or **one a half minutes** (Higher).

AQA GCSE French | Theme 2

2.2

WEDDINGS

À la mairie — At the town hall

1. Read Lola's account of a wedding she went to.

> Ma cousine Rose et son copain Abel se sont mariés l'été dernier et ils ont invité la famille et leurs amis. D'abord, on est allés à la mairie pour la cérémonie officielle. Ensuite, l'après-midi, la fête s'est passée dans le jardin d'un restaurant. On a bu, on a mangé, on a fait des jeux, on a écouté des discours. Le soir, il y avait de la musique et on a dansé. On s'est bien amusés !

Complete these sentences. Select the correct letter.

1.1 Rose and Abel got married …
   A last winter.
   B last summer.
   C last weekend.

1.2 The ceremony took place …
   A in a church.
   B at the town hall.
   C in the garden of a restaurant.

1.3 The party took place …
   A the next day.
   B the day before.
   C after the official ceremony.

1.4 There was food and drink and music, as well as …
   A fireworks.
   B candles and confetti.
   C games and speeches.

1.1 B   1.2 B   1.3 C   1.4 C.

s'amuser *to have a good time*	**Je m'amuse bien.** *I am having a good time.*	**Je me suis bien amusé / amusée.** *I had a good time*
se marier *to get married*	**Ils se marient.** *They are getting married.*	**Ils se sont mariés.** *They got married.*
se passer *to happen*	**Ça se passe en juin.** *It is happening in June.*	**Ça s'est passé en juin.** *It happened in June.*

+ Look at the table above for a reminder of how to use a **reflexive verb** in the present tense and in the perfect tense (**le passé composé**). See **page 155** for more details about reflexive verbs.

Les mariés — *The bride and groom*

Label this picture, using the French words below.

| le costume | les fleurs | la mariée |
| le marié | la cravate | la robe |

Dictation

2. You will hear **five** sentences, repeated **three** times (the first time as a full sentence, the second time in short sections and the third time again as a full sentence). Write them down in **French**.

2.1 Il y avait des fleurs partout. 2.2 Les invités ont félicité les mariés. 2.3 La mariée portait une belle robe longue. 2.4 Le marié portait un costume et une cravate. 2.5 Tout le monde a dansé jusqu'à deux heures du matin.

Make sure you understand each sentence, so you can re-use them in your own speaking and writing. Here is a translation: 2.1 *There were flowers everywhere.* 2.2 *The guests congratulated the bride and groom.* 2.3 *The bride was wearing a beautiful long dress.* 2.4 *The groom was wearing a suit and a tie.* 2.5 *Everyone danced until two o'clock in the morning.*

Note that on the Foundation paper, there are only **four** sentences.

Check you know the following prepositions to express when something happened.

avant la cérémonie	before the ceremony
pendant le repas	during the meal
après les discours	after the speeches
jusqu'à minuit	until midnight

3. Translate into **French**.
   3.1 We drank cocktails before the ceremony.
   3.2 Everyone was laughing during the speeches.
   3.3 The bride and groom started dancing after dessert.
   3.4 We partied until one o'clock in the morning.

3.1 On a bu / Nous avons bu des cocktails avant la cérémonie. 3.2 Tout le monde riait pendant les discours. 1.3 Les mariés ont commencé à danser après le dessert. 3.4 On a fait / Nous avons fait la fête jusqu'à une heure du matin.

2.2

CHRISTMAS TIME

Joyeux Noël !   *Merry Christmas!*

Label the pictures with the words below.

- les cadeaux
- les chocolats
- les décorations
- le repas
- le sapin

1. You read someone's thoughts about Christmas, posted in a forum. Answer the questions in **English**.

> Chez moi, Noël est très traditionnel. On a un beau sapin et des belles décorations. Le soir du 24 décembre, on mange un énorme repas et on boit du vin. Le 25 décembre, on ouvre les cadeaux qui sont sous le sapin. On mange souvent beaucoup de chocolats. Toute la famille est à la maison, on fait des jeux et c'est génial. Pourtant, je suis triste. Pourquoi ? Parce que je pense aux gens qui n'ont pas de maison, qui n'ont rien à manger. Je pense aussi aux gens qui sont malades ou qui sont seuls. Ça, ce n'est pas génial…

1.1 What is their house like at Christmas? Give **two** details.
1.2 What do they do on Christmas Eve? Give **two** details.
1.3 What do they do on Christmas day? Give **three** details.
1.4 Why are they sad? Give **four** details.

1.1 They have a Christmas tree and decorations. 1.2 They have an enormous meal and drink wine. 1.3 They open their presents and eat lots of chocolates. 1.4 They think about those who have no house, or who have nothing to eat. They think about those who are ill or alone.

! **Qui** is a relative pronoun that can be used to link up two parts of a sentence. It can be translated as *who*, *that* or *which*. How many examples of **qui** can you find in the text above?

2. Translate these sentences into **French**, using **qui** in each one.
   2.1 He often buys presents that are really expensive.
   2.2 I don't like Christmas trees that are too small or too big.
   2.3 We are going to eat the chocolates that are on the table.
   2.4 Christmas is difficult for people who don't have a family.

2.1 Il achète souvent des cadeaux qui sont vraiment chers. 2.2 Je n'aime pas les sapins de Noël qui sont trop petits ou trop grands. 2.3 On va manger / Nous allons manger les chocolats qui sont sur la table. 2.4 Noël est difficile pour les gens qui n'ont pas de famille.

Meilleurs vœux ! **Best wishes!**

3. You hear Anaïs, Hugo, Lola and Mahmoud talking about their opinion of Christmas. What does each person think?

   Write **P** for a positive opinion, **N** for a negative opinion, **P + N** for a positive and negative opinion.

   3.1 Anaïs P + N.   3.2 Hugo N.   3.3 Lola P.   3.4 Mahmoud P + N.

4. **H** You are writing to your French-speaking penfriend about what you think about Christmas.

   Write approximately **150 words** in **French**.
   You must write something about each bullet point.

   Mention:
   - how you normally celebrate and how you celebrated last year
   - what you like and don't like about Christmas.

   4. *Model answer: D'habitude, dans ma famille, on passe le jour de Noël chez mes grands-parents avec mes cousins et mes cousines. C'est un peu fou, mais on s'amuse bien. L'année dernière, ma grand-mère était malade, alors on est restés à la maison. On a décoré le sapin, comme d'habitude. Le matin de Noël, on a ouvert nos cadeaux et le chien s'est bien amusé avec tous les papiers ! On a téléphoné à ma grand-mère et on a tous chanté « Joyeux Noël ». Elle était vraiment contente. Notre voisine est venue partager notre repas de Noël, parce qu'elle n'a pas de famille.*

   Le 26 décembre, j'aime faire une longue promenade avec mes parents et le chien. Souvent, il fait très froid, mais je trouve ça sympa. Par contre, je pense que Noël, c'est trop compliqué. Il y a toujours des gens qui sont tristes ou malades ou énervants. C'est stressant. Je préfère célébrer les anniversaires, c'est plus facile.

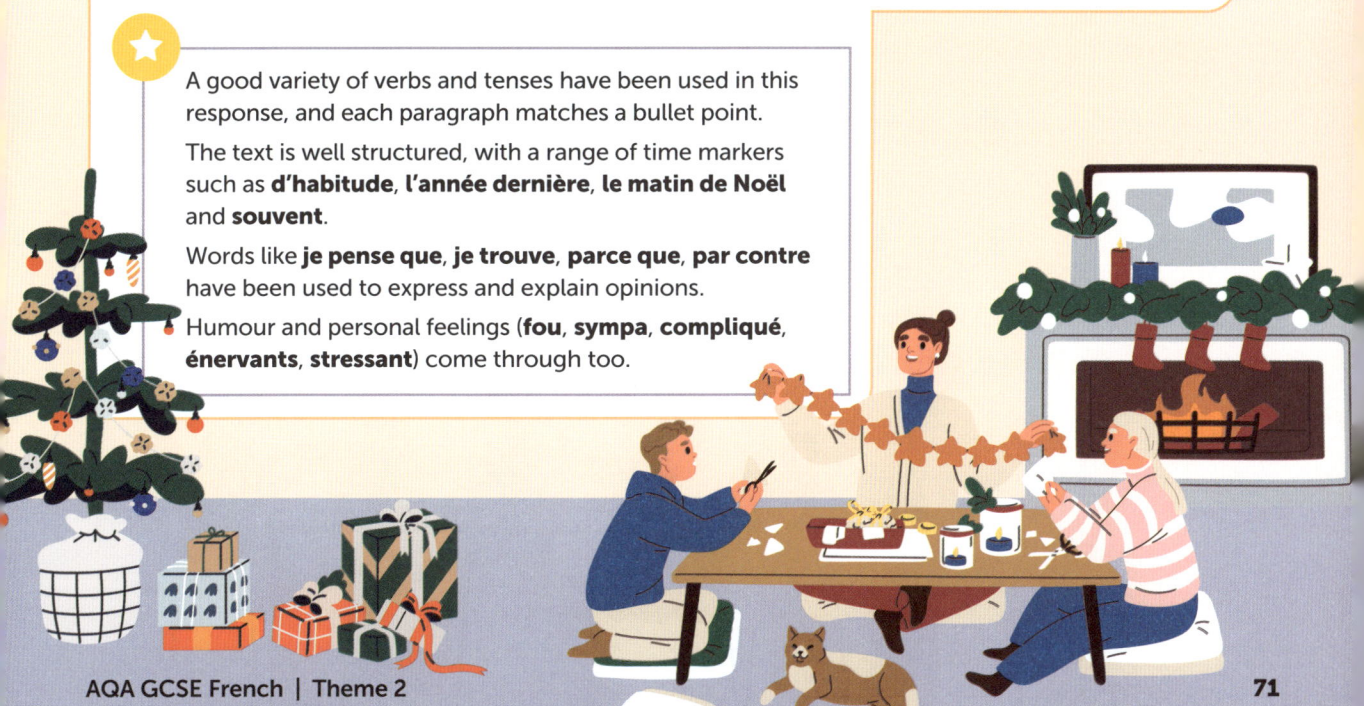

A good variety of verbs and tenses have been used in this response, and each paragraph matches a bullet point.

The text is well structured, with a range of time markers such as **d'habitude**, **l'année dernière**, **le matin de Noël** and **souvent**.

Words like **je pense que**, **je trouve**, **parce que**, **par contre** have been used to express and explain opinions.

Humour and personal feelings (**fou**, **sympa**, **compliqué**, **énervants**, **stressant**) come through too.

2.2

CUSTOMS, FESTIVALS AND CELEBRATIONS

Assemblage — *Putting it all together*

1. Read the following message from Lola to her friends.
   Write down whether the descriptions below refer to something happening now (**N**), something that happened in the past (**P**) or something that will happen in the future (**F**).

   > Coucou tout le monde,
   >
   > Comme d'habitude je passe les vacances de février avec ma tante et mon cousin. L'année dernière, on est allés faire du ski dans les Alpes – il y avait de la neige et c'était sympa. Mais cette année, c'est encore plus génial, car on est à Nice pour le Carnaval ! Tous les défilés sont vraiment fantastiques. Demain, on va aller voir la célèbre bataille des fleurs, et tout le monde dit que ce sera génial. Je vais vous envoyer des photos.

   1.1 Skiing
   1.2 Seeing snow
   1.3 Sending pictures
   1.4 Watching fantastic parades
   1.5 Being in Nice for the Carnival
   1.6 Going to watch the battle of the flowers parade
   1.7 Spending February half-term with relatives

   1.1 P   1.2 P   1.3 F   1.4 N   1.5 N   1.6 F   1.7 N

2. You hear a news item about Eid al-Fitr.
   Answer the questions in **English**.
   2.1 When will Eid al-Fitr start?
   2.2 How long will it last?
   2.3 How will Muslim families celebrate? (Give **three** details)

   2.1 tomorrow   2.2 three days   2.3 by sharing a big meal, offering presents, and eating delicious cakes

3. **F** Imagine you are Lola, sending a photo from Nice to your friends.
Write **five** sentences in **French** about the photo.

3. *Model response: 1. Je suis arrivée à Nice hier matin.   2. Le ciel est bleu et il fait très beau.
3. Aujourd'hui, c'est la bataille des fleurs.   4. Je passe des vacances de février fantastiques.
5. Je voudrais revenir avec vous l'année prochaine !*

4. **H** You are writing to your Canadian friend about a particular festival that you have attended or would like to attend.

Write approximately **150 words** in **French**.
You must write something about each bullet point.

Mention:
- what that festival is and when it takes place
- what you did on that day.

4. *Model response: L'été dernier, je suis allé en vacances en France et j'étais chez des amis français pour le 14 juillet, le jour de la fête nationale. On célèbre l'anniversaire de la Révolution française de 1789, quand le peuple a attaqué la prison de la Bastille à Paris. Maintenant c'est un jour férié, les Français ne travaillent pas, alors les gens sont de bonne humeur. Tout le monde veut faire la fête.*

    Le matin, à la télé, j'ai vu des défilés militaires sur les Champs Élysées et je n'ai pas trouvé ça très intéressant. Par contre, je me suis bien amusé le soir. Il y avait de la musique dans les rues et tout le monde dansait. À onze heures, on a vu un magnifique feu d'artifice sur la plage. Malheureusement, ça faisait beaucoup de bruit et le chien de mes amis a eu peur ! Moi, je voudrais y retourner l'année prochaine. Sans le chien !

> ⭐ In addition to being well written, this response shows the student knows about a specific aspect of French culture and history.

AQA GCSE French | Theme 2

2.3 CELEBRITIES

Mes préférés — *My favourites*

Choose the right words from the table below to label these pictures.

M	un	astronaute	acteur	chanteur	chef	footballeur	danseur
F	une	astronaute	actrice	chanteuse	cheffe	footballeuse	danseuse

! Make sure you know the masculine and feminine forms of jobs. Note that those ending in **e** in the masculine, like **astronaute**, don't change in the feminine.

Reading aloud

1. Read aloud this passage, then listen to the recording to check your pronunciation.

> Ma célébrité préférée est un chanteur belge. Je l'aime parce que sa musique est géniale. Ses chansons donnent envie de danser. Pourtant, elles parlent de choses importantes. Je voudrais rencontrer ce chanteur.

TRACK 50

Here is a translation of the text above so you can adapt some of it and use it in your speaking and writing tasks.

My favourite celebrity is a Belgian singer. I like him because his music is great. His songs make you want to dance. And yet, they talk about important things. I would like to meet this singer.

J'aime suivre …   *I like following …*

The French for *I follow / I am following* is **je suis**, which looks and sounds the same as **je suis** when it means *I am*. Only the context will tell you which one it is.

Luckily, there is no other overlap between these two verbs.

infinitive	suivre	être
present	je suis, tu suis, il / elle / on suit	je suis, tu es, il / elle / on est
perfect	j'ai suivi	j'ai été
imperfect	je suivais	j'étais
simple future	je suivrai	je serai
near future	je vais suivre	je vais être
conditional	je suivrais	je serais

! Look out for different forms of **suivre** in the reading task that follows.

2. You are reading an article in which three young people describe a celebrity they admire.

> **Maëlle Lakrar**
> Je m'intéresse à la footballeuse Maëlle Lakrar qui joue pour l'équipe de France depuis 2023. Née le 27 mai 2000, elle aime le foot depuis l'âge de six ans. Elle est très flexible et elle n'a pas peur de sortir de sa zone de confort pour aider son équipe. C'est pour ça que je la suis.
>
> **Mory Sacko**
> J'aime suivre un chef cuisinier français qui s'appelle Mory Sacko. On le connaît depuis 2020, quand il a participé à l'émission de télé « Top Chef ». Maintenant il anime une émission de télévision qui s'appelle « Cuisine ouverte ». Il a aussi un restaurant à Paris. Je le suis parce que ses plats ont des influences internationales : japonaises et africaines. Je trouve ça intéressant.
>
> **Thomas Pesquet**
> Je suis fasciné par l'astronaute Thomas Pesquet. Ses missions d'astronaute sont captivantes et il a passé un total d'environ 400 jours dans l'espace. Pourtant, il a d'autres activités intéressantes. Quand il n'est pas dans l'espace, il joue du saxophone, il joue au basket, il fait de la natation et beaucoup d'autres sports. En plus, il parle six langues. Son rêve : aller sur la Lune !

Match the correct person with each of the following questions.
Write **Ma** for Maëlle Lakrar, **Mo** for Mory Sacko, **T** for Thomas Pesquet.

2.1 Who likes swimming?   2.2 Who has a restaurant in Paris?
2.3 Who speaks several languages?   2.4 Who has their birthday in Spring?
2.5 Who presents a TV programme?

2.1 T   2.2 Mo   2.3 T   2.4 Ma   2.5 Mo

2.3

REALITY TV

Les émissions — *Programmes*

1. Read these comments about different TV reality programmes.

> Tout le monde sait que j'adore faire des gâteaux. Alors, je regarde souvent « Meilleur pâtissier » avec mon petit frère et j'ai appris beaucoup de choses intéressantes. En plus, ça m'a donné des nouvelles idées de gâteaux. Cette émission m'inspire.   **Anaïs**

> Quand je m'ennuie, je regarde « Star Academy ». Ça m'amuse de voir et d'écouter toutes ces personnes qui veulent devenir célèbres et gagner des prix. Il y a des candidats vraiment nuls. Mais parfois, certains candidats ont une très belle voix et beaucoup de talent.   **Mahmoud**

> Moi, j'ai regardé « Les apprentis aventuriers ». C'est une émission où les candidats sont sur une île déserte et ils doivent survivre dans des conditions difficiles. J'ai trouvé ça vraiment bête. Si les gens s'ennuient, ils peuvent aider dans une banque alimentaire. C'est plus utile !   **Hugo**

Complete these sentences. Select the correct letter.

1.1 The programme Anaïs often watches is about …
   A baking.
   B education.
   C brothers and sisters.

1.2 Mahmoud watches Star Academy when …
   A he wants to be famous.
   B he has nothing better to do.
   C he wants to listen to good music.

1.3 The programme Hugo watched takes place …
   A in an office.
   B in a food bank.
   C on a desert island.

1.4 Read Hugo's comments again. Instead of taking part in that reality TV show, what does Hugo suggest people do if they are bored?

1.1 A   1.2 B   1.3 C   1.4 They can help at a food bank.

Une bonne façon de se relaxer — A good way to relax

2. Translate these comments about reality TV programmes into **English**.

    2.1 Ces émissions sont nulles.
    2.2 C'est une bonne façon de s'amuser.
    2.3 Je trouve ce programme un peu bête.
    2.4 C'est une bonne façon de se relaxer avec ses amis.
    2.5 J'aime quand ma candidate préférée réussit.
    2.6 Je regarde cette émission quand je m'ennuie.
    2.7 Je regarde cette série quand j'ai besoin de rire.
    2.8 Je suis content quand mon candidat préféré gagne.
    2.9 Je ne suis pas content quand mon candidat préféré perd.

2.1 Those programmes are rubbish.   2.2 It is a good way of having fun.   2.3 I find this programme a bit silly.   2.4 It is a good way of relaxing with friends.   2.5 I like it when my favourite candidate succeeds.   2.6 I watch this programme when I am bored.   2.7 I watch this series when I need a laugh.   2.8 I am pleased when my favourite candidate wins.   2.9 I am not happy when my favourite candidate loses.

> Once you have checked the translations, rewrite those comments as two separate lists: one for what you regard as positive, one for what you see as negative.

Ce, **cet**, **cette** and **ces** are called demonstrative adjectives.

masculine singular	ce film	this/that film
masculine singular	cet acteur	this/that actor
feminine singular	cette série	this/that series
masculine or feminine plural	ces personnes	these/those people

Photo card

3. Look at the photo and make notes about it. Then set a timer and talk about it for about **45 seconds**. At the end, listen to the recording for a model answer.

TRACK 51

> To prepare for this task, have another look at all the language in this spread and adapt it.
>
> In the exam you will have to say something about two photos and talk for **one minute** (Foundation) or **one and a half minutes** (Higher).

2.3 CELEBRITIES AS ROLE MODELS

Les gens qui m'inspirent — *People who inspire me*

Make sure you know and can use these verbs.

abandonner	*to give up*
imiter	*to imitate*
avoir besoin de	*to need*
avoir envie de	*to feel like, to want to*

1. Translate these sentences into **English**.
   1.1 On a besoin de modèles.
   1.2 Ça nous donne plus d'énergie.
   1.3 Il ne va pas abandonner les langues.
   1.4 On a envie d'imiter les gens qu'on admire.
   1.5 Il y a des célébrités qui donnent le mauvais exemple.

   1.1 We need models. 1.2 It gives us more energy. 1.3 He is not going to give up languages.
   1.4 We feel like imitating the people we admire. 1.5 There are celebrities who set a bad example.

2. Listen to Anaïs and Hugo telling Lola what they think about role models. They make some of the following points. What **two** points does each person give? Write the correct letters.

   TRACK 52

A	Having a role model gives us energy.
B	Some celebrities set a bad example.
C	Being keen to imitate people we admire.
D	Sometimes needing inspiration to succeed.
E	Overestimating the importance of role models.
F	Finding someone who encourages us to do interesting things.

   2. Anaïs A, C; Hugo B, F

+ Read the transcript available online. Note down and learn phrases you can re-use.

Mon modèle — *My model*

3. Read what Mona says about her role model.

> Moi, mon modèle, c'est une athlète paralympique qui s'appelle Marie-Amélie Le Fur. Quand elle était petite, elle pratiquait l'athlétisme. Malheureusement, à l'âge de 16 ans, elle a eu un accident de la route et elle a perdu une jambe. Catastrophe ! Oui, mais elle n'a pas abandonné. En fait, elle a continué à faire du sport et elle a participé quatre fois aux Jeux Paralympiques. Elle a gagné beaucoup de médailles. Elle a aussi écrit des livres pour essayer de changer le regard sur le handicap. Elle m'inspire !

Answer the questions in **English**.
3.1 What sport did Marie-Amélie Le Fur practise as a child?
3.2 What happened to her when she was 16?
3.3 What did she do after that?
3.4 What does Mona say about her?

3.1 She practised athletics. 3.2 She had a road accident and lost a leg. 3.3 She didn't give up. She took part in the Paralympics and won a lot of medals. She has also written books to change the way people look at disability. 3.4 She is an inspiration.

Re-read the text above and pay attention to all the verbs. Find the following examples and check you understand how and why that particular tense has been used.
- Some are in the present tense (**c'est**, **elle s'appelle**, **elle m'inspire**).
- Others are in the imperfect to describe what Marie-Amélie was like (**elle était**) and what she used to do regularly (**elle pratiquait**).
- There are also verbs in the perfect tense to say what she did in the past (**elle a eu**, **elle a perdu**, **elle n'a pas abandonné**, **elle a continué**, **elle a participé**, **elle a gagné**, **elle a écrit**).

⊕ For more details about past tenses, go to **pages 150-151**.

4. Now translate these sentences into **French**, using the correct past tense.
   4.1 He was a great athlete.
   4.2 He won two medals last year.
   4.3 That victory gave us more energy.
   4.4 Recently, he wrote a book that inspired me.
   4.5 Before the accident he used to take part in all the competitions.

*4.1 C'était un athlète génial. 4.2 Il a gagné deux médailles l'année dernière.
4.3 Cette victoire lui a donné plus d'énergie. 4.4 Récemment, il a écrit un livre qui m'a inspiré.
4.5 Avant l'accident, il participait à toutes les compétitions.*

2.3

INFLUENCERS

Les célébrités du web — *Celebrities on the web*

1. You read this article about influencers.

> **Pourquoi est-ce qu'on est attiré par les influenceurs ?**
> Quand on est ado, on ne veut pas toujours écouter ses parents. On préfère les influenceurs parce qu'ils sont jeunes comme nous. Ils ont les mêmes problèmes que nous et ils s'intéressent aux mêmes choses que nous. C'est pour ça qu'on veut les suivre et écouter leurs recommandations.
>
> **Pourquoi est-ce qu'on doit faire attention ?**
> Certains influenceurs veulent gagner beaucoup d'argent. En plus, ils donnent souvent une fausse image de la réalité. Par exemple, ils nous font croire qu'on est nul si on n'a pas un corps parfait. Ça peut être dangereux pour la santé physique et mentale.

Answer the questions in **English**.
1.1 According to this article, what are the three reasons why young people like influencers?
1.2 What is the aim of some influencers?
1.3 What can be dangerous for physical and mental health?

1.1 They are young, have the same problems, and are interested in the same things as teenagers. 1.2 Earning a lot of money. 1.3 Making people think they are useless if they don't have a perfect body.

Remember that, in the present tense, the **ils / elles** form of verbs almost always ends in **-ent**. There are only four exceptions, where instead, the ending is **-ont**.

être	to be	je suis	ils / elles sont
avoir	to have	j'ai	ils / elles ont
faire	to make / do	je fais	ils / elles font
aller	to go	je vais	il / elles vont

Look for the **ils / elles** form of verbs in the passage above. How many can you spot?

On doit faire attention — *We have to be careful*

Make sure you know how to conjugate these three verbs in the present tense.

devoir must / to have to	pouvoir can / to be able to	vouloir to want
je dois	je peux	je veux
tu dois	tu peux	tu veux
il / elle / on doit	il / elle / on peut	il / elle / on veut
nous devons	nous pouvons	nous voulons
vous devez	vous pouvez	vous voulez
ils / elles doivent	ils / elles peuvent	ils / elles veulent

! Remember the verb that follows **devoir**, **pouvoir** and **vouloir** is always in the infinitive.
Tu dois faire attention. *You must be careful.*
Je peux être riche. *I can be rich.*
Tu ne veux pas réussir ? *Don't you want to succeed?*

Dictation

2. You will hear **five** sentences, repeated **three** times (the first time as a full sentence, the second time in short sections and the third time again as a full sentence). Write them down in **French**.

   2.1 Les jeunes admirent les influenceurs. 2.2 Ils veulent gagner beaucoup d'argent. 2.3 Ils n'ont pas envie d'écouter leurs parents. 2.4 Elles vont les suivre sur les réseaux sociaux. 2.5 On doit faire attention car ils peuvent être dangereux.

+ Make sure you understand each sentence, so you can re-use them in your own speaking and writing. Here is a translation:
2.1 *Young people admire influencers.*   2.2 *They want to earn a lot of money.*   2.3 *They don't want to listen to their parents.*
2.4 *They are to going to follow them on social media.*
2.5 *We / You must be careful because they can be dangerous.*

★ Note that on the Foundation paper, there are only **four** sentences.

3. Translate these sentences into **French**.
   3.1 I don't follow influencers.
   3.2 Everyone has to be careful.
   3.3 They also want to earn money.
   3.4 I can't be perfect, but I want to be healthy.
   3.5 Those influencers have the same problems as me.

*3.1 Je ne suis pas les influenceurs.   3.2 Tout le monde doit faire attention.   3.3 Ils veulent aussi gagner de l'argent.   3.4 Je ne peux pas être parfait / parfaite, mais je veux être en bonne santé.
3.5 Ces influenceurs ont les mêmes problèmes que moi.*

2.3 PROS AND CONS OF FAME

Tu veux être célèbre ? — *Do you want to be famous?*

What to say when you want to show two sides of an argument:

d'un côté	on the one hand
d'un autre côté	on the other hand
je ne suis pas sûr / sûre	I am not sure
je ne sais pas	I don't know
le pour et le contre	the pros and cons

! Listen out for those phrases in the listening task that follows.

1. Listen to Anaïs, Hugo, Lola and Mahmoud talking about being famous. What do they think of being famous?
   After each name, write **P** for a positive opinion, **N** for a negative opinion, or **P + N** for a positive and negative opinion.

   Anaïs   Hugo   Lola   Mahmoud

   TRACK 54

2. Listen again and add the missing words to complete these extracts.

   2.1 « On _____ porter des vêtements de _____ extraordinaires. C'est super ! »

   2.2 « La _____ est beaucoup plus intéressante. Moi, je _____ avoir une carrière internationale. »

   2.3 « Vous _____ être fous ! Quand on est célèbre on ne peut pas sortir quand on _____. »

   2.4 « On _____ faire attention parce que les gens critiquent facilement. Ça doit _____ fatigant. »

   1. Anaïs P, Hugo P, Lola N, Mahmoud P + N
   2.1 peut, marque.   2.2 vie, veux.   2.3 devez, veut.   2.4 doit, être.

Should, could and would

Now make sure you know these useful conditional forms of **devoir**, **pouvoir** and **vouloir**.

devoir	pouvoir	vouloir
must / to have to	*can / to be able to*	*to want*
je devrais	**je pourrais**	**je voudrais**
I would have to / I should	*I could*	*I would like to*

Si tu étais célèbre … — *If you were famous…*

3. Anaïs, Lola and Mahmoud are still talking about what it would be like to be famous.

Anaïs: Si j'étais célèbre, je pourrais voyager dans des pays exotiques et je pourrais rencontrer beaucoup de gens intéressants. Ce serait vraiment génial !

Lola: Si j'étais célèbre, je ne pourrais pas avoir de vie privée et je devrais faire attention à mon image. Ce serait trop stressant. Non, je ne voudrais pas être célèbre.

Mahmoud: Si j'étais célèbre, je pourrais changer le monde, mais je devrais faire face à plein de commentaires négatifs. Alors, je ne sais pas si je voudrais être célèbre.

Who mentions the following ideas? Write **A** for Anaïs, **L** for Lola, **M** for Mahmoud.

3.1 Lacking privacy
3.2 Putting up with criticism
3.3 Meeting interesting people
3.4 Travelling to fabulous places
3.5 Making a difference in the world
3.6 Worrying about the way they look

3.1 L   3.2 M   3.3 A   3.4 A   3.5 M   3.6 L

To talk about something that might never happen, use **si** + verb in the imperfect tense, followed by a verb in the conditional in the other part of the sentence.

si + imperfect	conditional
Si j'étais célèbre, … *If I was famous, …*	je n'aurais pas de vie privée. *I would not have any private life.*
Si j'avais beaucoup d'argent, … *If I had a lot of money, …*	j'essaierais d'aider les gens dans le besoin. *I would try to help people in need.*

For more details about the conditional, go to **page 154**.

---

4. **H** Translate into **French**.
   4.1 If I was famous, my life would be more difficult.
   4.2 If you were famous, you could live in a big house.
   4.3 If I was very rich, I would have to help people in need.
   4.4 If I didn't have a private life, I would find that stressful.
   4.5 If you had a lot of money, could you change the world?

4.1 Si j'étais célèbre, ma vie serait plus difficile.   4.2 Si tu étais célèbre, tu pourrais habiter/vivre dans une grande maison.   4.3 Si j'étais riche, je devrais aider les gens dans le besoin.   4.4 Si je n'avais pas de vie privée, je trouverais ça stressant.   4.5 Si tu avais beaucoup d'argent, est-ce que tu pourrais changer le monde ?

2.3

CELEBRITY CULTURE

Assemblage — *Putting it all together*

1. Listen to two candidates, Stella and Mick, on a reality TV show.
   They are talking about the reasons why they took part in the show.
   What **two** reasons does each candidate give? Write the correct letters.

   TRACK 55

A	Loving music
B	Becoming famous
C	Facing a challenge
D	Earning a lot of money
E	Travelling around the world
F	Meeting like-minded people

   1. Stella: C, F; Mick: A, E

2. 🖊 You and your friends are sharing photos on social media.
   What's in this photo? Write **five** sentences in **French**.

   2. Model response: 1. On est à un concert génial.   2. J'écoute ma chanteuse préférée qui joue de la guitare.   3. Je l'admire parce qu'elle a beaucoup de talent.   4. En plus, ses chansons sont très drôles.   5. Je voudrais être comme elle, car elle m'inspire.

Role play

3. Plan what you are going to say in this role play. Then play the recording and pause after you hear each question or statement, so you can give your response.
   When you see this **–?–** you will have to ask a question.

   You are talking to your French-speaking friend. Your friend will speak first.

   3.1 Say why you like your favourite celebrity. (Give **two** details).
   ? 3.2 Ask your friend a question about fame.
   3.3 Say how you normally follow celebrities.
   3.4 Give your opinion about influencers.
   3.5 Say what kind of TV programmes you watch and why.

TRACK 56

4. **H** You are writing to your Swiss friend about a celebrity you are following on social media.

   Write approximately **150 words** in **French**.
   You must write something about each bullet point.

   Mention:
   - who it is and what they do
   - whether you think you will continue to follow them in the future.

   4. Model response:
      Je m'intéresse à la chanteuse belge Angèle, qui a beaucoup de succès depuis plusieurs années. Pour commencer sa carrière, elle a publié ses vidéos en ligne. Je crois qu'elle a plus de trois millions d'abonnés sur Instagram. C'est fantastique ! On doit dire qu'Angèle vient d'une famille d'artistes. Son père est chanteur, sa mère est actrice et son frère est rappeur.

      Je suis cette chanteuse sur les réseaux sociaux parce que, à mon avis, elle a une très belle voix et un talent extraordinaire. Elle écrit elle-même les paroles et la musique de ses chansons. En plus, c'est une chanteuse engagée qui parle de choses sérieuses et importantes. Par exemple, elle veut se battre contre les discriminations. En même temps, elle fait tout ça avec beaucoup d'humour. C'est pour ça que j'adore l'écouter et regarder ses vidéos. J'espère vraiment qu'elle va continuer à chanter et faire des concerts très longtemps.

   + Once you have completed this writing task, have a look at the model response. Underline and make a list of words and phrases that you think work well. Then have another look at your own passage and see if you can improve it by using some of the words from your list.

   For example, you can introduce your opinion with phrases like **à mon avis**, **je crois que**, **j'espère que**. You can announce new ideas with phrases such as **en plus**, or **en même temps**.

KEY VOCABULARY

Students are expected to know 1200 items of vocabulary for Foundation tier and a further 500 for Higher tier. This list has some of the key vocabulary for Theme 2, but there are many more words listed in the AQA specification and in an interactive spreadsheet on the AQA website.

le cadeau	gift
le chanteur / la chanteuse	singer
la fête	party, festival
le gâteau	cake
la semaine	week
le vélo	bicycle
le vêtement	item of clothing, garment
amusant / amusante	amusing
dernier / dernière	last
joyeux / joyeuse	happy, merry, joyful
prochain / prochaine	next
triste	sad
à mon avis	in my opinion
aujourd'hui	today
demain	tomorrow
hier	yesterday
trop	too, too much / too many
vraiment	really
aller (je vais)	to go (I go / I am going)
devoir (je dois)	to have to (I must)
écouter	to listen to
faire attention (je fais attention)	to be careful (I am careful)
gagner	to win
jouer	to play
lire (je lis)	to read (I read / I am reading)
se passer	to happen
penser	to think

EXAMINATION PRACTICE

Popular culture – Reading

Read this text about Stella's birthday celebrations.

> Quand j'étais petite, je pouvais inviter huit amis à la maison. On regardait des dessins animés, on jouait et on mangeait le gâteau.
>
> Maintenant, j'essaie de faire quelque chose de différent tous les ans. L'année dernière, je suis allée à un match de foot avec mes amis. Notre équipe a gagné, alors l'ambiance était fantastique. On s'est bien amusés.
>
> Et pour mon prochain anniversaire ? Je cherche une idée originale.

Answer the following questions in **English**.

01 How did Stella celebrate her birthday when she was younger? Give **four** details. [4 marks]

02 What did she do last year? [1 mark]

03 Why did she and her friends have a good time? [1 mark]

04 What is she going to do for her next birthday? [1 mark]

Translate these sentences into **English**.

05 Ma cousine va se marier l'été prochain. [2 marks]

06 Mes parents disent que je sors trop souvent. [2 marks]

07 Il va regarder cette émission avec son meilleur ami. [2 marks]

08 Ils regardent le feu d'artifice depuis une demi-heure. [2 marks]

09 Si j'étais cheffe, je voudrais ouvrir un restaurant à Paris. [2 marks]

Popular culture – Listening

Voice messages

Your French friend has sent you some voice messages.

TRACK 57

A	Religion
B	Singing
C	Birthday
D	Celebrities
E	Bank holiday
F	TV programmes

What is each message about? Write the correct letter next to each idea.

01 Idea 1 _____ [1 mark]   03 Idea 3 _____ [1 mark]

02 Idea 2 _____ [1 mark]   04 Idea 4 _____ [1 mark]

Radio announcement

You hear this announcement on the local radio.

Write **A** if only statement A is correct, **B** if only statement B is correct, **A + B** if both statements A and B are correct.

TRACK 58

05 Today is … _____ [1 mark]
- **A** 21ˢᵗ of June.
- **B** World Music Day.

06 All concerts … _____ [1 mark]
- **A** are free.
- **B** will profit a charity.

07 There will also be a street dance … _____ [1 mark]
- **A** starting at 9 pm.
- **B** finishing at 9 pm.

Dictation

08 You will now hear **five** short sentences.

Listen carefully and, using your knowledge of French sounds, write down in **French** exactly what you hear for each sentence.

TRACK 59

You will hear each sentence **three** times: the first time as a full sentence, the second time in short sections and the third time again as a full sentence.

Use your knowledge of French sounds and grammar to make sure that what you have written makes sense. Check carefully that your spelling is accurate.

(Note that, on the **F** Foundation paper, there are only **four** sentences.) [10 marks]

Popular culture – Speaking

Reading aloud

01 **F** Read aloud the following text in **French** and then answer the questions in the recording.

> Je fête toujours mon anniversaire avec ma famille.
>
> J'aime aussi sortir avec mes amis.
>
> On va au cinéma ou on va voir un match de foot.
>
> Mon anniversaire, c'est ma fête préférée.

TRACK 60

You will be asked **four** questions in **French** that relate to the topic of customs, festivals and celebrations. In order to score the highest marks, you must try to answer all four questions as fully as you can.

Check your pronunciation by listening to the recording. Then listen to hear an example of a student answering the questions.

[5 + 10 marks]

Photo card

02 During your preparation time, look at the two photos. You may make as many notes as you wish and use these notes during the test.

02.1 You will be asked to talk about the content of these photos. The recommended time is roughly **one minute** for **F** Foundation Tier candidates and **one and a half minutes** for **H** Higher Tier candidates. You must say at least **one** thing about each photo. [5 marks]

TRACK 61

Photo 1

Photo 2

02.2 After you have spoken about the content of the photos, you will be asked questions related to any of the topics within the theme of popular culture. Listen to the recording. Pause after you hear each question and try to answer them in as much detail as possible.

TRACK 62

[20 marks]

AQA GCSE French

Popular culture – Writing

01 **(F)** You are sending an introduction email to a new penfriend.

Write approximately **50 words** in **French**.

You must write something about each bullet point.

Mention:
- your favourite pastime
- an activity you don't like
- your favourite type of film or TV programme
- your favourite celebrity
- your opinion about being famous. [10 marks]

---

02 **(F) + (H)** You are emailing your Belgian friend about celebrations.

Write approximately **90 words** in **French**.

You must write something about each bullet point.

Mention:
- what sort of celebrations you enjoy
- a recent family celebration you attended
- a celebration you are looking forward to in the coming months. [15 marks]

---

03 **(H)** You are writing a social media post about celebrities.

Write approximately **150 words** in **French**.

You must write something about both bullet points.

Describe:
- the celebrity you used to admire when you were a child
- what you would be like if you were a celebrity. [25 marks]

TOPICS FOR THEME 3
Communication and the world around us

Specification coverage

Topic 1 Travel and tourism, including places of interest
Topic 2 Media and technology
Topic 3 The environment and where people live

Information about the four papers for Foundation ⒻⒻ and Higher ⒽⒽ tiers:

Paper 1 – Listening

Written exam:
35 minutes Ⓕ, 45 minutes Ⓗ
40 marks Ⓕ, 50 marks Ⓗ
25% of GCSE

The recording is controlled by the invigilator with built-in repetitions and pauses.

Each exam includes 5 minutes' reading time at the start of the question paper before the listening material is played and 2 minutes at the end of the recording to check your work.

Section A – Listening comprehension questions in English, to be answered in English or non-verbally (Ⓕ 32 marks, Ⓗ 40 marks).

Section B – Dictation where students transcribe 4 sentences (Ⓕ 8 marks) or 5 sentences (Ⓗ 10 marks).

Paper 2 – Speaking

Non-exam assessment (NEA):
7–9 minutes Ⓕ or 10–12 minutes Ⓗ +
15 minutes' supervised preparation time
50 marks, 25% of GCSE

Role play – 10 marks, 1–1.5 minutes. Ⓕ Ⓗ

Reading aloud passage and short conversation – 15 marks.
Recommended time 2–2.5 minutes Ⓕ and 3–3.5 minutes Ⓗ.
Minimum 35 words Ⓕ and minimum 50 words Ⓗ.

Photo card discussion (two photos) – 25 marks.
Photo card discussion time:
4–5 minutes Ⓕ and 6–7 minutes Ⓗ.

Paper 3 – Reading

Written exam: 45 minutes Ⓕ, 1 hour Ⓗ
50 marks, 25% of GCSE

Section A – Reading comprehension questions in English, to be answered in English or non-verbally (40 marks).

Section B – Translation from French into English, minimum of 35 words Ⓕ or 50 words Ⓗ (10 marks).

Paper 4 – Writing

Written exam: 1 hour 10 minutes Ⓕ,
1 hour 15 minutes Ⓗ
50 marks, 25% of GCSE

Set of three short writing tasks. Ⓕ only. 25 marks.

Translation of sentences from English into French, minimum 35 words Ⓕ, or 50 words Ⓗ (10 marks).

Produce a piece of writing in response to three compulsory bullet points, approximately 90 words in total. Choose from two questions (15 marks). Ⓕ Ⓗ

Open-ended writing task.
Two compulsory bullet points, approximately 150 words in total. Choose from two questions. (25 marks). Ⓗ only.

TRANSPORTATION

3.1

Les moyens de transport — *Means of transport*

Choose the right words to label these pictures.

à pied	l'avion
le bateau	le bus
le métro	le train
le vélo	la voiture

Reading aloud

1. Read aloud the following text, then listen to the recording to check your pronunciation.

TRACK 63

> J'ai décidé de prendre un bus, parce que mon vélo est en panne. Il n'y avait pas de bus, alors je suis venu à pied. Je suis arrivé en retard et mes amis sont partis sans moi. En plus, j'ai perdu mon téléphone. C'est vraiment une mauvaise journée !

> **!** Pay attention to the pronunciation of **bus** and **en plus**: pronounce the final **s** but use a French **u** sound before it. Be careful with the **u** in **perdu** and **venu**. Remember that the **d** at the end of **pied** and **retard** is silent.

2. Translate the paragraph above into **English**.

> 2. I decided to take/get a bus because my bike doesn't work/has broken down. There was no bus, so I came on foot. I arrived late and my friends left without me. On top of that, I lost my phone. It really is a bad day!

Make sure you know the main forms of **prendre**, *to take*. Then **comprendre**, *to understand*, and **apprendre**, *to learn*, will be easy to remember as they follow the same patterns.

infinitive	present tense	perfect tense
prendre	je prends, tu prends, il / elle / on prend nous prenons, vous prenez, ils / elles prennent	j'ai pris

En retard ! *Late!*

3. Hugo has written this article about transport for the school newsletter.

> D'habitude, je prends mon vélo pour aller en ville. Je trouve ça pratique, même si c'est un peu dangereux. Il y a beaucoup de voitures dans les rues et je n'aime pas ça. Les bus et les métros sont plus écologiques. De temps en temps, je me dispute avec mes parents, parce que, à mon avis, ils prennent l'avion trop souvent. C'est mauvais pour la planète et le train est plus respectueux de l'environnement. Ma mère dit que l'avion est moins cher que le train et qu'il va plus vite. C'est peut-être vrai, mais je déteste les aéroports !

Answer the questions in **English**.

3.1 According to Hugo, what is the advantage and the disadvantage of riding a bike?
3.2 Why does Hugo argue with his parents?
3.3 What does Hugo's mother think of flying? Give **two** details.

3.1 It is convenient, but a little/a bit dangerous.   3.2 He thinks his parents fly too often.
3.3 She thinks it's quicker and less expensive than taking the train.

! Remember the use of **plus** *(more)* and **moins** *(less)* followed by an adjective or adverb.
C'est plus rapide. *It's quicker.*   **C'est moins cher.** *It's less expensive.*

4. Hugo is asking his friends, Anaïs, Lola and Mahmoud why they are all late! How did each person travel? Write the correct letter for each one.

TRACK 64

A	By bus
B	By car
C	By train
D	Cycled
E	On the underground
F	Flew
G	Walked

! Listen to the whole item before choosing your reply to a listening task. Here, for example, most of the speakers mention two means of transport: you need to work out which one to reject.

4.   Anaïs B, Lola C, Mahmoud G, Hugo D

5. Translate into **French**.
5.1 The train is often late.
5.2 Do you like travelling by boat? (Use **tu**.)
5.3 I waited for the bus, then I decided to go on foot.
5.4 In my opinion, taking the train is easier than the plane.

5.1 Le train est souvent en retard.   5.2 Tu aimes voyager en bateau ?   5.3 J'ai attendu le bus, puis j'ai décidé d'aller à pied.   5.4 À mon avis, prendre le train est plus facile que l'avion.

AQA GCSE French | Theme 3

3.1

THE WEATHER

Il fait quel temps ? — **What is the weather like?**

Here is a reminder of key phrases about the weather.

il fait froid	it is cold
il fait chaud	it is hot
il fait beau	the weather is nice
il pleut	it is raining
il neige	it is snowing
il y a du soleil	it is sunny
il y a du vent	it is windy

1. Anaïs and her friends are texting each other about the weather where they are. Which weather does each person mention? Write the correct letter by each name.

   Il a fait très froid hier et maintenant il neige.

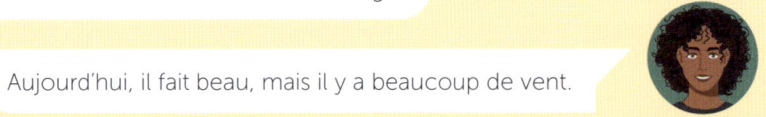

   Aujourd'hui, il fait beau, mais il y a beaucoup de vent.

   Demain, il va y avoir du soleil, mais il ne va pas faire très chaud.

A	clouds
B	rain
C	snow
D	sunshine
E	wind

   | Anaïs: |
   | Mahmoud: |
   | Lola: |

   1. Anaïs C, Mahmoud E, Lola D

Un temps changeant — *Changeable weather*

Remember to change the verb depending on whether you are talking about the weather now, in the past or in the future.

now	past		future	
present tense	perfect tense	imperfect tense	near future	future tense Ⓗ
il fait …	il a fait …	il faisait …	il va faire …	il fera …
il pleut	il a plu	il pleuvait	il va pleuvoir	il pleuvra
il neige	il a neigé	il neigeait	il va neiger	il neigera
il y a …	il y a eu …	il y avait …	il va y avoir …	il y aura …

2. Hugo is talking about the weather in the place where he is for half-term.

   Write **A** if only statement A is correct, **B** if only statement B is correct, **A + B** if both statements are correct.

   TRACK 65

   2.1 Yesterday, there was…
   A blue sky.
   B a lot of wind.

   2.2 Today…
   A it is colder.
   B it is warmer.

   2.3 Tomorrow's forecast is…
   A rain.
   B snow.

   2.4 Hugo thinks the weather is…
   A changeable.
   B wintry.

   2.1 A + B   2.2 B   2.3 A   2.4 A

3. Listen to the audio and answer the **four** questions in **French** related to the weather.
   Pause after each question to give your response.

   TRACK 66

   ! Pay attention to the tense used in the question. Is it in the present, the past or the future? Answer accordingly.

3.1

SCHOOL HOLIDAYS

Se relaxer *Relaxing*

1. Translate these sentences into **English**.
    1.1 Je dois faire mes devoirs.
    1.2 Tu peux profiter du soleil.
    1.3 Tu sais jouer du saxophone ?
    1.4 Elle veut faire la grasse matinée.
    1.5 Il voudrait aller voir ses grands-parents.

    1.1 I must do my homework.   1.2 You can make the most of the sun.   1.3 Can you play the saxophone?   1.4 She wants to sleep late.   1.5 He would like to go and see his grandparents.

+ To revise these useful modal verbs (**devoir**, **pouvoir**, **savoir** and **vouloir**), see **pages 156, 163, 165 and 166**.

2. You hear Anaïs talking about her and her friends' activities for today and tomorrow.

    Answer the questions in **English**.
    2.1 What was the weather like this morning?
    2.2 What is the weather forecast for tomorrow?

    Choose **A**, **B** or **C** to complete the sentences.
    2.3 Today Anaïs…
        A did her homework with Hugo.
        B went for a walk with Lola and Tommy.
        C went to the cinema with her brother and Mahmoud.
    2.4 Tomorrow Mahmoud …
        A will visit his grandparents.
        B will cook a meal for his family.
        C will go to the skatepark with his friends.

    2.1 It was raining   2.2 The weather will be good   2.3 C   2.4 B

TRACK 67

Vive les vacances ! — Long live the holidays!

The French equivalent of *by* or *while* + verb ending in *-ing* is **en** + present participle (a verb ending in **-ant** in French).

Je me relaxe en regardant une comédie. *I relax by watching a comedy.*
Je fais mes devoirs en écoutant de la musique. *I do my homework while listening to music.*

➕ For more details about the present participle, go to **page 155**.

3. You see a magazine article about relaxing during the school holidays.

> Nous avons demandé à six ados comment ils se relaxent pendant les vacances scolaires. Voici leurs réponses.
>
> « Je me relaxe...
>
> | | |
> |---|---|
> | A | en promenant mon chien. » |
> | B | en jouant à des jeux vidéo. » |
> | C | en écoutant de la musique. » |
> | D | en jouant au foot avec amis. » |
> | E | en faisant la grasse matinée. » |
> | F | en passant du temps avec mes copains. » |

Which answer matches each activity? Write the correct letter next to each one.

3.1 Sleeping late _____
3.2 Walking my dog _____
3.3 Listening to songs _____
3.4 Spending time with friends _____

3.1 E   3.2 A   3.3 C   3.4 F

4. 🅗 Translate into **French**.
   4.1 I often relax by staying at home.
   4.2 He learned French by watching French films.
   4.3 She is listening to music while preparing breakfast.
   4.4 Do you relax by playing video games with your friends? (use **tu** for *'you'*)
   4.5 They want to forget about the bad weather by going to the cinema.

4.1 Je me repose souvent en restant à la maison.   4.2 Il a appris le français en regardant des films français.   4.3 Elle écoute de la musique en préparant le petit-déjeuner.   4.4 Tu te relaxes en jouant à des jeux vidéo avec tes amis ?   4.5 Ils/Elles veulent oublier le mauvais temps en allant au cinéma.

AQA GCSE French | Theme 3

3.1 HOLIDAYS

Bonnes vacances ! **Have a good holiday!**

Find the correct caption for each picture.

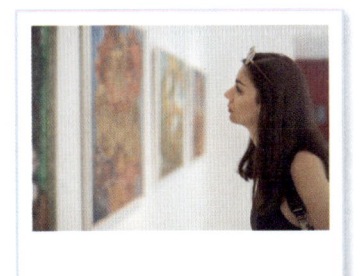

1. Sortir danser ? Oui, bien sûr !
2. C'est très important de bien se reposer.
3. Je voudrais aller à l'étranger l'été prochain.
4. Je vais aller voir une exposition dans un musée.
5. Faire du camping au bord de la mer, c'est génial !

1. You hear Lola talking about holidays. *TRACK 68*
   1.1 What does Lola say about her parents?
   1.2 What does she like about holidays spent at home? Give three details.
   1.3 What kind of holiday did she have with her friends? Give two details.

   1.1 They never go away on holiday. 1.2 They relax, sleep late and go out with Tommy, the dog.
   1.3 She went camping by the sea with friends, and that was great.

2. Read aloud the following text, then listen to the recording to check your pronunciation. *TRACK 69*

   Je suis au bord de la mer avec ma famille. Hier matin, nous sommes allés à la plage parce qu'il faisait très chaud. Par contre, l'après-midi, il a commencé à pleuvoir, alors nous avons visité le musée d'art moderne. Et toi ? Tu passes de bonnes vacances ?

3. Translate the paragraph in question 2 into **English**.

> 3. I am at the seaside with my family. Yesterday morning, we went to the beach because it was very hot. However, it started raining in the afternoon, so we visited the modern art museum. What about you? Are you having a good holiday?

Partir ou rester à la maison ? — Going away or staying at home?

Use the conditional form of a verb to say what would happen. The conditional has the same stem as the future tense and the same endings as the imperfect.

infinitive	imperfect	simple future	conditional	
aller	j'allais	j'irai	j'irais	*I would go*
avoir	il y avait	il y aura	il y aurait	*there would be*
être	c'était	ce sera	ce serait	*it would be*
faire	il faisait	il fera	il ferait	*it would be / make*
neiger	il neigeait	il neigera	il neigerait	*it would snow*

Il neigerait et il ferait froid. J'irais dans les montagnes, ce serait fantastique !
It would snow and it would be cold. I would go to the mountains, it would be fantastic!

4. Use the words listed below to complete Lola's text about her ideal holiday.

> Mes vacances idéales ? J'_____ sur une île tropicale avec mes amis. Il y _____ du soleil et il _____ beau, mais pas trop chaud. Je _____ dans la mer tous les jours et je _____ du surf. En plus, on _____ au volley. Le soir, on _____ dehors et on _____ de la musique. Je m'_____ bien. Si tout ça était possible, ce _____ vraiment génial !

amuserais	aurait	écouterait	ferais	ferait
irais	jouerait	mangerait	nagerais	serait

4. irais, aurait, ferait, nagerais, ferais, jouerait, mangerait, écouterait, amuserais, serait.

PLACES OF INTEREST

Vacances en France   *A holiday in France*

1. You see an advert for a region to visit during a holiday in France.

   Venez passer vos vacances en Ardèche !

   On peut faire du canoë-kayak en passant sous l'arche du Pont d'Arc. C'est magique ! On peut aussi visiter la grotte Chauvet 2 et admirer des répliques de peintures préhistoriques. C'est fascinant ! Vous préférez les randonnées ? Allez marcher dans le parc naturel régional des Monts d'Ardèche. C'est magnifique !

   Et n'oubliez pas Balazuc, un des plus beaux villages de France. Dans ce petit village très pittoresque, il n'y a pas beaucoup de magasins, mais il y a un musée d'histoire naturelle et une plage pour nager dans la rivière. C'est sympa, l'été !

   Complete these sentences. Select the correct letter.

   1.1 People go to the Chauvet 2 cave to…
      A hire a canoe.
      B dance on the bridge.
      C see prehistoric paintings.

   1.2 The Monts d'Ardèche park will appeal to people who like…
      A skiing.
      B hiking.
      C skating.

   1.3 Balazuc is the name of…
      A another river.
      B a prehistoric park.
      C one the most beautiful villages in France.

   1.4 In Balazuc, you can also…
      A go shopping.
      B swim in the river.
      C go to the swimming pool.

   1.1 C   1.2 B   1.3 C   1.4 B

C'était comment ? *What was it like?*

> ⭐ The exam usually includes listening and reading tasks that describe a part of France or a French-speaking region. Use this spread to get familiar with language and information that will help you with this type of task. It can also help you with writing and speaking.

Most adjectives in French come after the noun they describe. However, some common and very useful adjectives come before the noun: they include **grand / grande**, **petit / petite**, **bon / bonne**, **mauvais / mauvaise**, **beau / belle**, **joli / jolie**. Look at them in these examples:

une petite ville moderne   *a small modern town*
un joli village touristique   *a pretty, touristy village*
une grande ville industrielle   *a big industrial city*
une belle grotte préhistorique   *a beautiful prehistoric cave*

2. You hear Anaïs asking Mahmoud about his recent trip to Morocco.
   For each question and answer, which aspect of the trip is mentioned?
   Write the correct letter for each number (1–4).

A	airport
B	buying local products
C	small town
D	swimming pool
E	trip to the mountains
F	weather

   TRACK 70

3. 🎧 Listen again and answer the questions.
   3.1 Who did Mahmoud stay with?
   3.2 What did they buy at the market? Give **three** details.

   2.1 C   2.2 F   2.3 E   2.4 B
   3.1 with friends of his parents   3.2 (delicious) olives, sandals, a leather bag

4. Translate into **French**.
   4.1 I live in a small historical town.
   4.2 We visited the natural history museum.
   4.3 You can go on beautiful walks in the area.
   4.4 There is no beach, but there is a swimming pool.
   4.5 We are going to spend our holiday in the south of the country.

   4.1 J'habite dans une petite ville historique.   4.2 Nous avons/On a visité le musée d'histoire naturelle.   4.3 On peut / Tu peux / Vous pouvez faire de belles randonnées dans la région.   4.4 Il n'y a pas de plage, mais il y a une piscine.   4.5 Nous allons/On va passer nos vacances dans le sud du pays.

AQA GCSE French | Theme 3

3.1

TRAVEL, TOURISM AND PLACES OF INTEREST

Assemblage — *Putting it all together*

1. You see some headings in a French magazine.

   A Les musées à visiter cet été

   B Bien préparer ses voyages à l'étranger

   C Profitez des vacances pour faire la grasse matinée

   D Partir en randonnée en famille : le bon équipement

   E Dix conseils pour bronzer sans danger

   Which heading matches each idea? Write the correct letter next to each one.

   1.1 Hiking _____

   1.2 Sunbathing _____

   1.3 Sleeping late _____

   1.1 D   1.2 E   1.3 C

Dictation

2. You will hear **five** sentences, repeated **three** times (the first time as a full sentence, the second time in short sections and the third time again as a full sentence).

   Write them down in **French**.

   TRACK 71

   *2.1 J'ai pris mon vélo hier.   2.2 Il a commencé à pleuvoir.   2.3 Elle voudrait faire du camping.
   2.4 Aujourd'hui, il fait beau mais il y a du vent.   2.5 Je me relaxe en jouant au foot avec mes amis.*

   + Make sure you understand each sentence, so you can re-use them in your own speaking and writing. Here is a translation:
   2.1 *I took my bicycle yesterday.*   2.2 *It started to rain.*
   2.3 *She would like to go camping.*   2.4 *Today the weather is nice, but it is windy.*   2.5 *I relax by playing football with my friends.*

   ★ Note that on the Foundation paper, there are only **four** sentences.

Photo card

3. Look at the photo and make notes about it. Then set a timer and talk about it for about **45 seconds**. At the end, listen to the recording for a model answer.

To prepare for this task, have another look at all the language in this spread and adapt it.

sauter = *to jump*

---

4. You are writing an article about your area for a French website.

Write approximately **90 words** in **French**.
You must write something about each bullet point.

Describe:
- the main places of interest in your area
- a recent event you and your friends enjoyed in your area
- something fun that will happen next year in your area.

4. Model response:
J'habite dans une petite ville au bord de la mer, dans l'ouest de la France. Alors, on peut s'amuser sur la plage. Il y a aussi beaucoup de magasins intéressants et des cafés où on peut manger des glaces délicieuses.

L'été, on peut assister à un festival de musique sur le port. L'année dernière, j'y suis allé/allée avec mes amis et on a écouté des groupes extraordinaires.

L'année prochaine, il va y avoir un grand championnat de skate et je voudrais y participer. Si je m'entraîne bien, je gagnerai peut-être !

3.2

USING A SMARTPHONE

Mon téléphone — *My phone*

Here are some key phrases relating to your phone.

appeler les parents	to call parents
écouter de la musique	to listen to music
envoyer des messages	to send messages
jouer à des jeux	to play games
prendre des photos	to take photos
regarder des vidéos	to watch videos
partager des photos	to share photos
utiliser des applis	to use apps

1. You hear Anaïs and Mahmoud talk about their phones.
   Who did what today? Write **A** for Anaïs, **M** for Mahmoud and **A + M** for both. *(TRACK 73)*

   1.1 Discussed homework _____

   1.2 Listened to music _____

   1.3 Sent messages _____

   1.4 Spoke to a family member _____

   1.5 Took photos _____

   1.6 Paid in a shop _____

2. 🎧 Listen again and answer the questions.

   2.1 What does Anaïs find annoying? _____

   2.2 What homework does Mahmoud mention? What is the problem with it? _____

1.1 M   1.2 A + M   1.3 A   1.4 A   1.5 M   1.6 M
2.1 Her mother often calls her to know where she is.   2.2 Maths homework. It is difficult.

Mon appli préférée — *My favourite app*

Do not confuse the verb **je préfère**, *I prefer*, with the adjective **préféré**, favourite. The two words sound different (note the accents).

The ending of the verb will change depending on who does the action. Here are all the present tense forms of the verb:

je préf**è**re   tu préf**è**res   il/elle/on préf**è**re   nous préf**é**r**ons**   vous préf**é**r**ez**   ils/elles préf**è**r**ent**

The adjective **préféré** needs to agree with the noun it goes with:

masculine singular	feminine singular	masculine plural	feminine plural
mon jeu préféré *my favourite game*	ma chanson préférée *my favourite song*	mes jeux préférés *my favourite games*	mes chansons préférées *my favourite songs*

Dictation

3. You will hear **five** sentences, repeated **three** times (the first time as a full sentence, the second time in short sections and the third time again as a full sentence). Write them down in **French**. Note that on the Foundation paper, there are only **four** sentences.

3.1 Je préfère regarder des vidéos amusantes. 3.2 Je vais partager mes photos préférées avec toi. 3.3 Je joue à mon jeu préféré tous les jours après l'école. 3.4 Mon appli préférée est utile pour écouter de la musique. 3.5 Il n'aime pas téléphoner et il préfère envoyer un message.

Check you know the main direct object pronouns and remember that, unlike in English, they come before the verb.

masculine singular	le /l'	him, it
feminine singular	la/l'	her, it
masculine and feminine plural	les	them

You also know the French for 'me' – **me/m'**, and 'you' – **te/t'**.
Ma mère m'appelle. *My mother is calling me.*
Quelle vidéo marrante ? Je voudrais la voir. *What funny video? I would like to see it.*

4. Translate into **French**.
   4.1 My mother often calls me to know where I am.
   4.2 When it's a good photo, I send it to my grandfather.
   4.3 I watch funny videos and I share them with my friends.
   4.4 I know my Spanish vocabulary because I revise it with an app.
   4.5 My favourite songs are on my phone, and I listen to them all the time.

*4.1 Ma mère m'appelle pour savoir où je suis.   4.2 Quand c'est une bonne photo, je l'envoie à mon grand-père.   4.3 Je regarde des vidéos marrantes et je les partage avec mes amis.
4.4 Je sais mon vocabulaire d'espagnol parce que je le révise avec une appli.
4.5 Mes chansons préférées sont sur mon téléphone et je les écoute tout le temps.*

THE INTERNET

C'est pratique — It's handy

Here are some key words and phrases relating to your phone.

acheter	to buy
une appli	app
faire des recherches	to research
en ligne	online
télécharger	to download
trouver des infos	to find information
utile	useful
vendre	to sell

1. Lola has written an article on how she uses the internet in her daily life.

> J'utilise internet tous les jours, et j'ai du mal à imaginer la vie autrement. Le matin je me réveille avec la radio en ligne. Ils passent de la musique qui me donne de l'énergie. Ça m'aide à être de bonne humeur le matin !
>
> Internet, c'est utile pour le travail scolaire. On peut communiquer avec les profs et les autres élèves de la classe. On peut faire des recherches et trouver des infos. On peut aussi télécharger des applis comme Quizlet pour faire ses révisions, ou Duolingo pour apprendre son vocabulaire d'espagnol.
>
> Je n'aime pas vraiment aller dans les magasins et je préfère acheter – et vendre ! – mes vêtements en ligne. Ça aussi, c'est pratique !

Answer the questions in **English**.

1.1 What does Lola do to wake up in the morning?
1.2 What effect does it have on her?
1.3 How does the internet help with schoolwork? Give **three** details.
1.4 According to Lola, what can you do to help with revision or learn your Spanish vocab?
1.5 How does Lola usually buy her clothes? Why?

1.1. She uses an online radio station that plays music.   1.2 It puts her in a good mood in the morning.   1.3 She can communicate with her teachers and classmates; she can do research and find information.
1.4 You can download apps.
1.5 Lola usually buys her clothes online because she doesn't like going to shops.

C'est vraiment utile — *It's really useful*

2. Read aloud the following text, then listen to the recording to check your pronunciation.

TRACK 75

> Mon père dit que je télécharge trop d'applis sur mon téléphone, mais je trouve ça pratique. Quand j'ai besoin d'infos, je fais des recherches sur internet. C'est vraiment utile pour faire mes devoirs. J'utilise aussi internet pour envoyer des emails à ma grand-mère, car elle n'a pas de téléphone portable.

+ Although we don't normally pronounce consonants at the end of French words (as in **dit**, **trop**, **applis**, **quand**, **infos**, and so on), you will hear the **t** at the end of **internet** because it is a word adopted into French from English. Also note the pronunciation of **des emails**; you need to link up those two words with a **z** sound.

3. Translate the paragraph above into **English**.

> 3. My father says that I download too many apps on my phone, but I find it useful. When I need information, I do some research on the internet. It is really useful for doing my homework. I also use the internet to send emails to my grandmother, because she doesn't have a mobile phone.

4. You are listening to Anaïs and Hugo talking about applications they have downloaded.

TRACK 76

Write **A** if only statement A is correct, **B** if only statement B is correct, **A + B** if both statements are correct.

4.1 Anaïs uses an app to…
   A buy clothes.
   B sell clothes.

4.2 Anaïs thinks that using that app helps…
   A save money.
   B save the planet.

4.3 Hugo has downloaded an app to…
   A improve his language skills.
   B do muscle-building exercises.

4.4 Hugo thinks this application is good but…
   A he hasn't started using it yet.
   B he only uses it ten minutes a day.

4.1 A + B   4.2 A + B   4.3 A   4.4 B

AQA GCSE French | Theme 3

3.2

SOCIAL MEDIA

Utiliser les réseaux sociaux — *Using social media*

Reading aloud

1. Read aloud this passage, then listen to the recording to check your pronunciation.

TRACK 77

> Généralement, les ados utilisent beaucoup les réseaux sociaux. Ils discutent souvent avec leurs amis et leur famille. Ils aiment être créatifs quand ils partagent des photos et des vidéos. Ils s'amusent vraiment.

! Be careful when you come across a word ending in **-ent**. The **-ent** is silent when it is part of a verb in the **ils/elles** form (such as **utilisent**, **discutent**, **aiment**, **partagent**, **s'amusent**). But when it is another word, such as an adverb (**généralement**, **souvent**, **vraiment**), the **-ent** is pronounced as a separate syllable. Listen and repeat with care when you say those words.

2. Translate the paragraph above into **English**.

> 2. *Usually, teenagers use social media a lot. They often chat with their friends and their family. They like being creative when they share photos and videos. They really enjoy themselves!*

3. You hear this online item about French teenagers and social networks.

   Select the correct answer to each question.

   TRACK 78

   3.1 With the most popular social media platforms, teenagers…
   - **A** cannot share music.
   - **B** can only send word messages.
   - **C** can easily share photos and videos.

   3.2 Teenagers can be creative by…
   - **A** sending short messages.
   - **B** deleting their messages quickly.
   - **C** adding fun filters to their messages.

   3.3 The teenagers in this recording like Snapchat because…
   - **A** messages do not stay long.
   - **B** they can use it to follow celebrities.
   - **C** nobody else can read their messages.

   3.4 They say they feel the way Snapchat works…
   - **A** is very addictive.
   - **B** protects their privacy.
   - **C** stops them from overusing the app.

   3.1 C   3.2 C   3.3 A   3.4 B

Facilement — *Easily*

Many French adverbs end in **-ment** (in the same way as many English adverbs end in **-ly**). Listen again to the listening task from **page 108**.

a) Which of the following adverbs do you hear in it?

1	extrêmement
2	facilement
3	généralement
4	particulièrement
5	rapidement
6	vraiment

b) Now match up those French adverbs 1–6 with their English equivalents:

easily   extremely   particularly   quickly   really   usually

a) Answers: 2, 5, 6
b) Answers: 1. extremely   2. easily   3. usually   4. particularly   5. quickly   6. really

---

4. Complete the following sentences in **French**. Choose the correct word from the three options, as shown in the example below.

Example: On peut envoyer des messages ___rapidement___.
   particulièrement   rapidement   vêtement

4.1 On peut utiliser des filtres _____ amusants.
   lentement   rapidement   vraiment

4.2 Ma copine envoie des messages _____ créatifs.
   extrêmement   harcèlement   comment

4.3 Qu'est-ce que tu fais _____ sur les réseaux sociaux ?
   complètement   généralement   moment

4.4 Avec les réseaux sociaux, je communique _____ avec mes amis.
   aiment   facilement   relativement

4.1 vraiment   4.2 extrêmement   4.3 généralement   4.4 facilement

---

! Note! Many adverbs end in **-ment**, but not all words ending in **-ment** are adverbs!

TECHNOLOGY PROBLEMS

C'est énervant ! *It's annoying!*

Use the following vocabulary to help you answer the questions on this page.

un écran	screen
casser	to break
laisser tomber	to drop
oublier	to forget
perdre	to lose
voler	to steal

1. Translate these sentences into **English**.
   1.1 Je n'ai plus de batterie.
   1.2 Ne perds pas ton portable !
   1.3 Il a oublié son portable dans le bus.
   1.4 On a volé mon portable au festival de musique.
   1.5 Son écran est cassé parce qu'elle a laissé tomber son téléphone.

   1.1 I have run out of battery.   1.2 Don't lose your mobile!   1.3 He forgot his mobile on the bus. 1.4 Someone stole my mobile at the music festival.   1.5 Her screen is broken because she dropped her phone.

2. You hear Anaïs and her friends talking about their phones.

   2.1 Who mentions what? Write the correct letter for each person.

   TRACK 79

   Anaïs:  _____   Hugo:  _____   Lola:  _____   Mahmoud: _____

   | A | No credit | C | Parents nagging | E | Running out of battery |
   | B | A broken screen | D | Mobile got stolen | F | Dropping phone in a river |

   2.2 🎧 Listen to Mahmoud again. Why was he particularly annoyed?

   2.1 Anaïs B, Hugo C, Lola E, Mahmoud F
   2.2 He was without a phone for five weeks.

Ça ne marche pas — *It doesn't work*

3. You read these messages about technology by Anaïs and her friends.

« Quand je suis chez moi, j'ai parfois besoin de communiquer avec les profs ou avec les élèves de ma classe. C'est stressant quand l'internet ne marche pas ! » **Anaïs**

« Moi, je n'aime pas utiliser l'ordinateur pour faire mes devoirs. Je préfère les écrire à la main. » **Hugo**

« J'ai souvent mal aux yeux, alors je n'ai pas toujours envie de regarder un écran d'ordinateur. Je préfère sortir avec mon chien. » **Lola**

« Mon collège est bien équipé avec plein de tablettes et de tableaux interactifs. Mais de temps en temps, il y a un gros problème informatique et rien ne marche. C'est presque drôle ! » **Mahmoud**

Complete these sentences. Select the correct letter.

3.1 Anaïs finds it stressful when she needs to contact her teacher or classmates but …
   A she has no computer.
   B she can't find her mobile.
   C the internet at home isn't working.

3.2 Hugo prefers to write his homework …
   A by hand.   B on his mobile.   C on the computer.

3.3 Lola doesn't always want to look at computer screens because …
   A she gets nauseous.
   B she often gets sore eyes.
   C she gets frequent headaches.

3.4 Mahmoud almost finds it funny when, at school …
   A they can work in teams.
   B all the tablets are switched on.
   C there is a big IT failure, and nothing works.

3.1 C   3.2 A   3.3 B   3.4 C

Role play

4. You are talking to your French-speaking friend about using the internet. Your friend will speak first. When you see this **–?–** you will have to ask a question.
   4.1 Say what you like doing online. (Give **two** details).
   4.2 Talk about **one** app you have downloaded.
   4.3 Say what you find annoying about technology.
   ? 4.4 Ask your friend **one** question about the internet.
   4.5 Mention **one** thing other members of your family do online.

TRACK 80

3.2

THE IMPACT OF TECHNOLOGY

Attention à la technologie *Be careful with technology*

1. Read these thoughts about cybersecurity in a magazine.

   La technologie, c'est utile, mais il faut faire attention à certaines choses.

   La sécurité :
   N'oubliez pas de protéger votre vie privée en contrôlant qui peut voir vos publications.

   Le cyberharcèlement :
   Si vous recevez des messages horribles, il est important d'en parler à un adulte.

   La dépendance :
   Si on passe trop de temps devant son écran, on finit par avoir des problèmes de santé et de concentration. N'oubliez pas de sortir avec vos amis et votre famille ou d'aller courir au parc !

   La pression sociale :
   Sur les réseaux sociaux, il est facile de faire des comparaisons et de penser qu'on est moins bien que les autres. Ce n'est pas vrai ! Chaque personne est unique, avec ses propres qualités.

   Answer the questions in **English**.
   1.1 According to this article, what should you do if you are bullied online?
   1.2 What does the article advise you to do to get away from the screen? Give **two** details.
   1.3 How do they suggest you protect your privacy?
   1.4 What is the final point made in the article?

   1.1 Talk about it to an adult.   1.2 Go out with your friends and family or go for a run in the park.
   1.3 By controlling who can see your posts.   1.4 Beware of social pressure! Everyone is unique and has their own qualities.

When to use **c'est** + adjective and when to choose **il est** + adjective?

When the phrase stops after the adjective, use **c'est**.

When the adjective is followed by **de** + infinitive, you can use **il est**.
Il est interdit d'utiliser votre téléphone en classe. *It's forbidden to use your phone in class.*
C'est énervant. *That's annoying!*

Qu'est-ce qu'il faut faire ? — *What do you have to do?*

> **!** Remember you can use **il faut** + infinitive, instead of **tu dois** or **vous devez**, when you are giving general advice.
> **Il faut écouter.** *You have to listen.*
> **Il faut se protéger.** *You have to protect yourself.*

2. You hear Anaïs and her friends summarising the article from **page 112**. What does each person talk about? Write the correct letter for each name.

TRACK 81

Anaïs:  _____   Hugo:  _____   Lola:  _____   Mahmoud: _____

A	Cyberbullying	C	Passwords	E	Social pressure
B	Dependency	D	Privacy	F	Viruses

2. Anaïs A   Hugo D   Lola E   Mahmoud B

3. Translate into **French** with **Il faut** + infinitive.
    3.1 You have to be careful.
    3.2 You have to protect your privacy.
    3.3 You have to speak to an adult if you have a problem.
    3.4 You have to go out with your friends from time to time!
    3.5 You have to limit the time you spend in front of a screen.

3.1 Il faut faire attention.   3.2 Il faut protéger ta vie privée.   3.3 Il faut parler à un adulte si tu as un problème.   3.4 Il faut sortir avec tes amis de temps en temps !   3.5 Il faut limiter le temps que tu passes devant un écran.

3.2

MEDIA AND TECHNOLOGY

Assemblage — *Putting it all together*

1. You see this advert online.

   Vous voulez apprendre une langue étrangère ?

   Téléchargez l'appli AIDOLINGO.

   Avec AIDOLINGO, on peut :
   - réviser le vocabulaire
   - comprendre la grammaire
   - écouter et lire des histoires amusantes
   - parler en faisant attention à la prononciation

   Avec AIDOLINGO, on progresse en s'amusant !
   Tout simplement !

   Complete these sentences. Write the letter for the correct option.

   1.1 AIDOLINGO is an app you can download if you want to …
       A write funny stories.
       B learn a foreign language.
       C submit your homework on time.

   1.2 With that app you can …
       A make videos.
       B watch foreign films.
       C understand grammar and learn vocabulary.

   1.3 You can also …
       A speak to your friends.
       B do your history homework.
       C improve your pronunciation.

   1.4 AIDOLINGO claims you can make progress…
       A while having fun.
       B with public speaking.
       C even if you don't use it regularly.

   1.1 B   1.2 C   1.3 C   1.4 A

> **!** Always make sure you understand everything you read. Then make a note of useful phrases so you can adapt and reuse them for your own writing and speaking tasks.

2. **H** Write a short article about the main advantages of the internet, in your opinion. Write approximately **150 words** in **French**. You must write something about each bullet point.

   Say:
   - what you think it is good for and use it for
   - how other members of your family use the internet

   Model response: Je ne peux pas imaginer la vie sans internet. C'est pratique pour mon travail scolaire, car j'utilise internet pour faire des recherches et pour contacter mes profs et les autres élèves de ma classe. Je télécharge aussi beaucoup de musique, c'est essentiel pour moi. En plus, grâce à internet, je suis sur les réseaux sociaux et je communique avec mes amis en envoyant des messages et en partageant des photos et des vidéos. Je fais ça presque tous les jours !

   Ma petite sœur joue à des jeux en ligne. Je faisais ça avant, mais maintenant je préfère sortir. Mes parents utilisent aussi internet pour leur travail et pour envoyer des emails, chercher des recettes de cuisine et faire du shopping en ligne. Ils disent aussi que c'est bien pour télécharger des films. Je suis d'accord que c'est probablement utile, et je devrais essayer de faire ça plus souvent.

   ! Notice this student has used other parts of the verb besides **je**. They have also used other tenses – the imperfect tense, **en** + present participle and the conditional – to increase variety and complexity.

Photo card

3. Look at the photo and make notes about it. Then set a timer and talk about it for about **45 seconds**. At the end, listen to the recording for a model answer.

TRACK 82

3.3

WHERE PEOPLE LIVE

Chez moi   *At home*

1. Read what Anaïs says about her new house, and spot each of the words listed in the table.

   > J'ai une nouvelle maison ! Au rez-de-chaussée, il y a la cuisine, le séjour, les toilettes et l'escalier pour monter au premier étage. Là, il y a la salle de bains et deux chambres. Je suis en train de ranger ma chambre qui est au deuxième étage. J'ai une belle vue sur le jardin, alors c'est assez sympa.

le rez-de-chaussée	ground floor
le premier étage	first floor
la cuisine	kitchen
le séjour	living room
la chambre	bedroom
la salle de bains	bathroom
l'escalier	stairs
le jardin	garden

   + Using **être en train de** + infinitive is a neat way to say you are doing something right now, you are 'in the middle of doing x'.

   Je suis en train de faire mes devoirs. *I am in the middle of doing my homework.*

2. Now listen to Anaïs comparing her previous home and the new one.

   Select the correct answer to each question.

   TRACK 83

   1.1 Anaïs used to live…
   - **A** in a village.
   - **B** in a flat in the suburbs.
   - **C** in a flat in the town centre.

   1.2 Her home was…
   - **A** on the third floor.
   - **B** on the ground floor.
   - **C** on the thirteenth floor.

   1.3 There was no garden, but…
   - **A** they had a cellar.
   - **B** they had flowers on the balcony.
   - **C** there was a park opposite the flat.

   1.4 They now have a garden and…
   - **A** a garden shed.
   - **B** a garage for their car.
   - **C** a garage to keep their bicycles.

   1.1 C   1.2 A   1.3 B   1.4 B

Dans ma chambre — *In my bedroom*

Use the words below to label this picture.

- des étagères — shelves
- une chaise — chair
- des rideaux — curtains
- la fenêtre — window
- un mur — wall
- le lit — bed
- un tapis — rug
- une lampe — lamp
- une table — table

3. Translate into **French**.

   3.1 My flat is close to the station.
   3.2 I have lived here for six months.
   3.3 I would like to live in a house at the seaside
   3.4 I like my bedroom because it is comfortable.

   3.1 Mon appartement est près de la gare.   3.2 J'habite ici depuis six mois.   3.3 Je voudrais vivre dans une maison au bord de la mer.   3.4 J'aime ma chambre parce qu'elle est confortable.

4. Listen to the audio and answer the four questions in **French** related to your home. Pause after each question to give your response. Try to answer all questions as fully as you can.

   TRACK 84

AQA GCSE French | Theme 3

TOWNS AND CITIES

En ville   *In town*

1. Listen to a conversation between Anaïs and her friends, Hugo, Lola and Mahmoud. Which two places in town does each person mention? Write **two** letters for each name.

TRACK 85

Anaïs: _____

Hugo: _____

Lola: _____

Mahmoud: _____

A	bank
B	bridge
C	café
D	cinema

E	factory
F	hospital
G	library
H	market

I	school
J	shopping centre
K	stadium
L	station

1.   Anaïs J, C   Hugo G, D   Lola A, F   Mahmoud L, K

Reading aloud

2. Read aloud this passage, then listen to the recording to check your pronunciation.

TRACK 86

> Je ne suis pas très loin de la gare. Continue jusqu'au bout de la rue. Avant le pont, tourne à gauche. Il y a un magasin de journaux en face de la banque. Je t'attends au café qui est derrière le magasin.

! Always be careful with words that look like English words. They very rarely sound the same in French and in English. When listening to the recording, pay particular attention to words such as **continue**, **tourne**, **magasin**, **face**, **banque** and **attends**. Try to reproduce the pronunciation as closely as you can.

3. Translate the paragraph above into **English**.

3.   *I am not very far from the station. Continue to the end of the road. Before the bridge, turn left. There is a newspaper shop opposite the bank. I am waiting for you at the café that is behind the shop.*

118   ClearRevise

Devant le château — *In front of the castle*

> **!** Make sure you know all these words expressing position before continuing.

à côté de	next to
au bout de	at the end of
derrière	behind
devant	in front of
en face de	opposite
loin de	far from
près de	near

3. Translate into **French**.
   4.1 The shop is in front of the old castle.
   4.2 I see many tourists on the bridge.
   4.3 There is a small café near the river.
   4.4 Is the restaurant next to the museum?
   4.5 We would like to visit this historical place.

   4.1 Le magasin/La boutique est devant le vieux château.   4.2 Je vois beaucoup de touristes sur le pont.   4.3 Il y a un petit café près de la rivière.   4.4 (Est-ce que) le restaurant est à côté du musée ?   4.5 On voudrait visiter cet endroit historique.

Photo card

4. Look at the photo and make notes about it. Then set a timer and talk about it for about **45 seconds**. At the end, listen to the recording for a model answer.

TRACK 87

3.3

DESCRIBING THE AREA

Là où j'habite   *Where I live*

1. You read these messages by Anaïs and her friends about the area where they live. Which of these aspects get positive comments (P), and which get negative ones (N)?

« J'aime bien ma ville, car il y a plein de bons magasins et d'endroits sympas pour s'amuser. Par contre, je crois qu'il faut améliorer les transports. Il n'y a pas assez de bus et de métros. C'est dommage ! » **Anaïs**

« Mon père dit qu'il n'y a pas assez de parkings en ville. Je ne suis pas d'accord. À mon avis, le centre-ville devrait être interdit aux voitures. Il y a trop de pollution ! » **Hugo**

« Là où j'habite, il y a beaucoup d'espaces verts et des parcs avec des beaux arbres. C'est vraiment agréable. Et mon chien Tommy est d'accord avec moi ! » **Lola**

« Il y a beaucoup d'endroits pour faire du sport près de chez moi : une piscine, un stade, un skate-park, c'est génial. Le problème, c'est que les rues ne sont pas propres. Il y a trop de déchets par terre et c'est horrible ! » **Mahmoud**

1.1 Cleanliness _____

1.2 General entertainment _____

1.3 Green spaces _____

1.4 Parking _____

1.5 Sport facilities _____

1.6 Transport links _____

1.1 N   1.2 P   1.3 P   1.4 N   1.5 P   1.6 N

Find each of the words from the grid in the text above, and make sure you learn them.

améliorer	to improve
les déchets	rubbish
un endroit	place
interdit	banned
par terre	on the ground
propre	clean

La ville ou la campagne ? — Town or country?

C'est très animé.	It's very lively.
C'est vraiment calme.	It's really quiet.
Il n'y a rien à faire.	There is nothing to do.
Il y a beaucoup de bruit.	It's very noisy.
Il y a beaucoup de pollution.	There is a lot of pollution.
L'air est pur.	The air is clean.
On s'amuse bien.	We have fun.
On s'ennuie.	We are bored.

+ Rewrite these phrases as two separate lists: one for what you regard as positive, and another for what you regard as negative.

2. You hear Anaïs and her friends talking about the advantages and disadvantages of living in the country. Who expresses the following views?

   For each question, write **A** for Anaïs, **H** for Hugo, **L** for Lola, or **M** for Mahmoud.

   Who…

   2.1 dislikes the countryside? _____

   2.2 hasn't decided what is best? _____

   2.3 thinks you get the best of both worlds in a town? _____

   2.4 would like to live in the countryside in the future? _____

   2.1 H   2.2 A   2.3 M   2.4 L

3. **H** You are writing to your French-speaking penfriend about whether you would rather live in a town or in the country.

   Write approximately **150 words** in **French**.
   You must write something about each bullet point.
   Say:
   - where you live and what you like about it.
   - what life is like in a different place and whether you would like to live there.

   3. *Model response:*

   Moi, pour l'instant, j'habite dans un petit village à la campagne. J'aime bien là où j'habite, parce que c'est calme et l'air est pur. J'ai un chien et on fait de belles promenades tous les jours. En plus, je passe beaucoup de temps avec mes amis car ils habitent près de chez moi. On s'amuse bien ensemble.

   Quand j'étais petit/petite, j'habitais en ville. Il y avait beaucoup de bruit et beaucoup de pollution et j'étais souvent malade. À la campagne, l'air est pur et on respire mieux. Alors, c'est meilleur pour la santé ! Quand je vais en ville, c'est plus facile d'aller au cinéma et à des concerts. Il y a toujours des magasins et des cafés sympas et beaucoup de choses à faire. On ne s'ennuie jamais ! Pourtant, je ne voudrais pas être en ville tout le temps. Je crois que, dans l'avenir, je resterai vivre à la campagne.

3.3

THE ENVIRONMENT

Sauve la planète ! *Save the planet!*

1. Look at this list of suggestions to help the environment.

   1.1 Achète des vêtements d'occasion
   1.2 Consomme moins
   1.3 Cultive tes légumes
   1.4 Économise l'eau
   1.5 Éteins la lumière en quittant une pièce
   1.6 Ne laisse pas d'ordures par terre quand tu es dehors
   1.7 Plante des arbres
   1.8 Recycle tout ce que tu peux
   1.9 Trie les ordures et choisis la bonne poubelle
   1.10 Utilise les transports en commun

Find the right translation for each item in the list of advice above.
A. Plant trees
B. Save water
C. Consume less
D. Use public transport
E. Grow your vegetables
F. Buy second-hand clothes
G. Recycle everything you can
H. Switch off the light when leaving a room
I. Sort the rubbish and choose the right bin
J. Don't leave rubbish on the ground when you are outside

1.1 F   1.2 C   1.3 E   1.4 B   1.5 H   1.6 J   1.7 A   1.8 G   1.9 I   1.10 D

When telling someone what to do, or giving advice, you are using a verb in the imperative form.
To make the imperative, start from the present tense, remove the pronoun (**tu**) and remove the final **-s** if it is an **-er** verb. For more details about the imperative, go to **page 154**.

Present tense	Imperative
tu recycles *you recycle*	**recycle** *recycle*
tu éteins *you switch off*	**éteins** *switch off*
tu choisis *you choose*	**choisis** *choose*

Protège l'environnement ! *Protect the environment!*

Reading aloud

2. Read aloud this passage, then listen to the recording to check your pronunciation.

> Il est important de protéger l'environnement. Alors, j'utilise souvent mon vélo ou les transports en commun. En plus, je vais essayer d'économiser l'eau et l'électricité. Je voudrais aussi manger moins de viande et cultiver des légumes dans le jardin de mes parents.

! When listening to the recording, pay particular attention to the pronunciation of **l'environnement**, **j'utilise**, **d'économiser**, **l'eau**, **l'électricité**. Those pairs of words are pronounced as one word, as if there was no apostrophe.

3. Translate the paragraph above into **English**.

> 3. It is important to protect the environment. That's why I often use my bicycle or public transport. In addition, I am going to try to save water and electricity. I would also like to eat less meat and grow vegetables in my parents' garden.

4. You hear Hugo asking Anaïs, Lola and Mahmoud for their ideas to protect the environment.

Write **A** if only statement A is correct, **B** if only statement B is correct, **A + B** if both statements A and B are correct.

4.1 Anaïs ...
   A is going to grow vegetables in her new garden.
   B has been growing vegetables with her brother.

4.2 Lola ...
   A usually switches the light off when leaving a room.
   B is going to switch off her computer every night.

4.3 Mahmoud ...
   A has been recycling old clothes.
   B is going to buy second-hand clothes.

4.1 A   4.2 A + B   4.3 B

AQA GCSE French | Theme 3

OUR PLANET

La crise climatique — *Climate crisis*

These words and phrases are important if you want to talk or write in French about the climate crisis, so try to learn them. Find each one in the text below.

une abeille	bee
la chaleur	heat
les combustibles fossiles	fossil fuels
les émissions de gaz à effet de serre	greenhouse gas emissions
un équilibre	balance
une inondation	flood
la production alimentaire	food production
la sècheresse	drought
la tempête	storm

1. You read this article about climate change.

   Quelle est la cause principale du changement climatique ?
   Ce sont les émissions de gaz à effet de serre (comme le CO_2).

   Et d'où viennent ces émissions de gaz à effet de serre ?
   C'est parce qu'on utilise des combustibles fossiles pour avoir de l'électricité et de la chaleur.

   Il y a d'autres raisons ?
   Il y a aussi la production industrielle, la déforestation, l'utilisation de transports comme les voitures ou les avions et la production alimentaire.

   Pourquoi est-ce que c'est inquiétant ?
   Parce que c'est la cause de catastrophes, comme les sècheresses, les tempêtes et les inondations. Certaines régions du monde disparaîtront sous l'eau.

   Et la biodiversité ?
   La biodiversité est essentielle pour protéger l'équilibre de la planète. Par exemple, si les abeilles disparaissent, les humains disparaîtront aussi. Notre planète est en danger !

   Answer the questions in **English**.
   1.1 According to the article, what is the main reason for climate change?
   1.2 What causes greenhouse gas emissions? (Give **five** causes.)
   1.3 What are the **three** examples of natural disasters mentioned in the article?
   1.4 According to the article, what will happen to some parts of the world?
   1.5 What will happen if bees disappear?

   1.1 greenhouse gas emissions   1.2 the use of fossil fuels, industrial production, deforestation, transport such as cars and planes, and food production, 1.3 droughts, storms, floods, 1.4 they will disappear under water, 1.5 humans will disappear too.

La crise climatique continued

2. Hugo mentions four kinds of actions that help tackle the climate crisis. What is each one about? Listen and write the correct letter (1–4).

   TRACK 91

A	Planting trees
B	Repairing things
C	Protecting bees
D	Reducing rubbish
E	Saving natural resources
F	Developing renewable energy

   2.1 B   2.2 A   2.3 F   2.4 E

3. Translate these sentences into **English**.
   3.1 Les abeilles ne doivent pas disparaître.
   3.2 Les ressources naturelles sont essentielles.
   3.3 On doit réparer les objets au lieu de les jeter.
   3.4 Nous voulons tous protéger l'environnement.
   3.5 L'énergie solaire est une énergie renouvelable importante.

   3.1 Bees must not disappear.   3.2 Natural resources are essential.   3.3 We must repair things instead of throwing them away.   3.4 We all want to protect the environment.   3.5 Solar energy is an important renewable energy.

Dictation

4. You will hear **five** sentences, repeated **three** times (the first time as a full sentence, the second time in short sections and the third time again as a full sentence).

   Write them down in **French**. Note that on the Foundation paper, there are only **four** sentences.

   TRACK 92

   *4.1 On a besoin de planter plus d'arbres.   4.2 Il est important de protéger l'environnement.
   4.3 Nous devons réparer les objets au lieu de les jeter.   4.4 Il est nécessaire d'économiser les ressources naturelles.   4.5 On devrait développer les énergies renouvelables, comme l'énergie solaire.*

> **!** Bear in mind that when two verbs follow each other in French, the second one is in the infinitive. The verb is also in the infinitive when it comes after a preposition such as **à** or **de**.

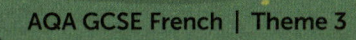

THE ENVIRONMENT AND WHERE PEOPLE LIVE

Assemblage — Putting it all together

1. You see this article about Lausanne in Switzerland.

Lausanne, meilleure petite ville du monde

Quand on arrive à Lausanne, en Suisse, on admire immédiatement le lac Léman, les montagnes et les vignes*. Le paysage est magnifique ! Avec 350 hectares de parcs et de jardins, Lausanne est une ville verte et agréable. On peut se promener à pied, ou on peut prendre les transports publics : bus, métro, train ou bateau, vous avez le choix !

Quoi faire à Lausanne ? C'est comme vous voulez. C'est une ville universitaire très animée. En centre-ville, le quartier du Flon vous offre des magasins, cafés et restaurants dans une zone principalement piétonne. En plus de la très belle cathédrale, vous y trouverez toujours quelque chose d'intéressant à visiter. Si vous aimez le sport, allez donc au musée olympique.

Bonne visite !

*les vignes   *vineyards*

Answer the questions in **English**.

1.1 What do people see when they arrive in Lausanne? Give **three** details.
1.2 Why is Lausanne a nice place to visit?
1.3 What is the choice of public transport in Lausanne?
1.4 What museum do they recommend you visit?

1.1 The lake, mountains and vineyards.   1.2 Wonderful landscape, with cathedral, parks and gardens / lively, green and pleasant city.   1.3 walking, bus, metro, train or boat.
1.4 The Olympic museum.

! Pay attention to the structure of this article and make a note of useful phrases such as **quand on arrive**, **vous avez le choix**, **quoi faire**, **bonne visite!** Then try to re-use them in your own article about the city or region where you live.

2. You are writing a post about the environment on social media.

   Write approximately **90 words** in **French**.
   You must write something about each bullet point.
   Say:
   - why you are concerned
   - what you are doing in your school to help the environment
   - what other things you are going to do, personally, to save the planet.

   2. Model response:
   La crise climatique est inquiétante et c'est la cause de catastrophes, comme les tempêtes et les inondations. Nous devons faire quelque chose pour protéger la planète.

   Dans mon collège, nous n'utilisons plus de bouteilles en plastique et nous avons créé un compost. En plus, on nous encourage à venir au collège à vélo.

   Moi, personnellement, j'aime la mode, mais j'achète surtout des vêtements d'occasion. J'ai discuté avec ma famille et nous allons faire deux choses : devenir végétariens et arrêter de prendre l'avion. J'espère que ça va être possible !

Photo card

3. Look at the picture and make notes about it. Then set a timer and talk about it for about **45 seconds**. At the end, listen to the recording for a model answer.

TRACK 93

Theme 3

KEY VOCABULARY

Students are expected to know 1200 items of vocabulary for Foundation tier and a further 500 for Higher tier. This list has some of the key vocabulary for Theme 3, but there are many more words listed in the AQA specification and in an interactive spreadsheet on the AQA website.

un avion	aeroplane
le bord de la mer	seaside
le bruit	noise
la campagne	countryside
la chambre	bedroom
les déchets / les ordures	rubbish
un écran	screen
le métro	tube, underground
la plage	beach
la pollution	pollution
les réseaux sociaux	social media
le soleil	sun
les vacances	holiday
la ville	town
la voiture	car
chaud / chaude	warm, hot
facile	easy
froid / froide	cold
propre	clean
sale	dirty
utile	useful
à l'étranger	abroad
en retard	late
acheter	to buy
envoyer	to send
neiger	to snow
partager	to share
partir (je pars)	to leave (I leave/I am leaving)
perdre	to lose
pleuvoir (il pleut)	to rain (it rains/it is raining)
protéger	to protect
recycler	to recycle
télécharger	to download
vendre	to sell

Theme 3

EXAMINATION PRACTICE

Communication and the world around us – Reading

You read comments that people have written about where they live.

01 Mon appartement est au troisième étage. On a un balcon et une belle vue sur le parc. Malheureusement, les voisins ne sont pas très sympas et ils font beaucoup de bruit. **Abel**

02 Nous sommes en ville, dans une petite maison. Mon quartier est dans une zone piétonne, et il y a un grand parc près de chez moi. C'est vraiment agréable parce que c'est très vert. En plus, c'est très pratique car il y a un arrêt de bus en face de ma maison. **Béa**

03 J'habite ici depuis trois mois et j'espère ne pas rester longtemps. Je m'ennuie, car il n'y a pas beaucoup de choses à faire. En plus, il y a beaucoup de déchets dans les rues. **Mario**

04 La ville où j'habite est très jolie ; il y a une belle rivière et des musées intéressants à visiter. Ce qui est difficile, c'est qu'il y a beaucoup de touristes et tout est très cher. **Sonia**

What do they think about where they live? Write **P** for a positive opinion, **N** for a negative opinion, **P + N** for a positive and negative opinion. (01–04) [4 marks]

You read this article giving the writer's views about where it's best to live.

Quand j'étais petite, j'habitais dans une maison de village. On pouvait faire de belles promenades, mais le village était loin de tout. On avait constamment besoin de la voiture : pour aller à l'école, pour aller au supermarché ou pour voir nos amis. C'était énervant !

Maintenant, j'habite en ville dans un petit appartement. Le quartier est très animé, mais il y a beaucoup de bruit. Il y a vraiment plus de pollution qu'à la campagne. À cause de ça, je suis souvent malade.

Dans l'avenir, je voudrais vivre dans une maison à la campagne, sans pollution. J'aimerais avoir un grand jardin pour cultiver des fruits et des légumes. L'idéal serait un endroit calme, mais pas complètement isolé du reste du monde. J'ai besoin d'un arrêt de bus près de la maison ; comme ça, ce serait facile d'aller en ville pour retrouver mes amis.

Answer the following questions in **English**.
05 Where did the writer live as a child? [1 mark]
06 What was annoying about living there? (Give **two** details.) [2 marks]
07 Where does she live now? (Give **two** details.) [2 marks]
08 Why does she often get ill? [1 mark]
09 Where would she like her next house to be? (Give **two** details.) [2 marks]
10 How would she manage to meet up with her friends? [1 mark]

AQA GCSE French

Communication and the world around us – Listening

You hear some young people talking about apps they want to use.

A	bus travel
B	health and fitness
C	jokes
D	mental health
E	selling clothes
F	weather forecast

TRACK 94

What is each one for? Write the correct letter.

01 Adèle _____ [1 mark]

02 Noah _____ [1 mark]

03 Esther _____ [1 mark]

04 Selim _____ [1 mark]

Esther has left a voicemail for her mother while on holiday with her friend Adèle's family. Write the correct number for Esther's activity. Also write the correct letter for when it takes place.

TRACK 95

1	Playing basketball	P	Past
2	Reading a book	N	Now
3	Swimming	F	Future
4	Visiting a castle		

05 Activity: _____ When: _____ [2 marks]

06 Activity: _____ When: _____ [2 marks]

Dictation

07 You will now hear **five** short sentences.

Listen carefully and, using your knowledge of French sounds, write down in **French** exactly what you hear for each sentence.

You will hear each sentence **three** times: the first time as a full sentence, the second time in short sections and the third time again as a full sentence.

TRACK 96

Use your knowledge of French sounds and grammar to make sure that what you have written makes sense. Check carefully that your spelling is accurate.

(Note that, on the ❻ Foundation paper, there are only **four** sentences.) [10 marks]

Communication and the world around us – Speaking

Role play

You are speaking to your French-speaking friend. Plan what you are going to say, taking into account the number of details you will need. Then play the recording, pausing after each question or statement so you can give your response. When you see this: –?– you will have to ask a question.

TRACK 97

In order to score full marks, you must include a verb in your response to each task.

- 01 Say how you prefer to travel and why.
- 02 Say where went on holiday recently and what you liked about it. (Give **two** details).
- 03 Say how like to use technology when you are on holiday.
- ? 04 Ask your friend **one** question about holidays.
- 05 Mention **two** things about the area where you would like to live in the future. [10 marks]

Reading aloud

06 Read aloud the following passage and then answer the questions in the recording. [5 + 10 marks]

> J'habite dans une petite ville au bord de la mer. C'est très agréable en hiver, mais il y a beaucoup de touristes en été. Quand il fait beau, je vais au collège à vélo. Par contre, quand il pleut, j'utilise une appli pour savoir à quelle heure arrive le bus. C'est pratique !

TRACK 98

07 During your preparation time, look at the two photos. You may make as many notes as you wish and use these notes during the test.

TRACK 99

Photo 1

Photo 2

You will be asked to talk about the content of these photos. The recommended time is approximately **one minute** for ❶ Foundation Tier candidates and **one and a half minutes** for ❽ Higher Tier candidates. You must say at least **one** thing about each photo. [5 marks]

08 Now answer the recorded questions for the unprepared conversation. [20 marks]

TRACK 100

AQA GCSE French

Communication and the world around us – Writing

You and your French-speaking friends are sharing photos on Snapchat.

01 **F** What is in this photo? Write **five** sentences in **French**. [10 marks]

02 **F** + **H** Translate the following sentences into **French**.
- 02.1 Turn off the light.
- 02.2 Yesterday I went to town by car.
- 02.3 It is essential to protect the planet.
- 02.4 I am going to spend my holiday abroad next year.
- 02.5 We have started to grow vegetables in the garden. [10 marks]

03 **H** You are writing a social media post about the ideal town.
Write approximately **150 words** in **French**.
You must write something about both bullet points.

Describe:
- what you like and don't like about where you live now
- what your ideal place would be like in the future. [25 marks]

GRAMMAR

The grammar requirements for GCSE are set out in two tiers: Foundation and Higher.

Students are required to use their knowledge of grammar from the specified lists, appropriate to the relevant tier of entry.

Students completing Higher tier assessments will be required to apply all grammar listed for Foundation tier in addition to the grammar listed for ❿ Higher tier.

Grammar

NOUNS AND ARTICLES

Nouns

Nouns are words used to name a thing, person or place. Examples: 'book', 'teacher', 'house'. It often helps to ask yourself if a word can have 'the' before it. If it can, it is a noun ('the book', 'the teacher', 'the house').

All French nouns (words to name people, places or things) are either masculine or feminine. When you learn new nouns, make sure you know whether they are masculine or feminine.

Masculine	
le frère	the brother
un frère	a brother
le cinéma	the cinema
un cinéma	a cinema
le vélo	the bike
un vélo	a bike

Feminine	
la sœur	the sister
une sœur	a sister
la table	the table
une table	a table
la voiture	the car
une voiture	a car

Nouns ending in **-ité** are feminine:
une activité activity
la nationalité nationality
une université university

Nouns ending in **-ion** are feminine:
la circulation traffic
la région region
la télévision television
One exception: **un avion** aeroplane

In French, a verb in the infinitive is sometimes used as a noun.
The English equivalent is the **-ing** form of the verb.
Fumer est mauvais pour la santé. *Smoking is bad for your health.*

Many names of jobs have a masculine and a feminine version.

Masculine	Feminine	
-eur	-eure / -euse / -rice	
un professeur	une professeure	teacher
un danseur	une danseuse	dancer
un directeur	une directrice	director
-ien	-ienne	
un pharmacien	une pharmacienne	pharmacist
-ier	-ière	
un infirmier	une infirmière	nurse

Plurals of nouns

As in English, most French nouns have plurals ending in **-s**.
Les professeurs et les élèves. *The teachers and the students.*

There are exceptions:
Words ending in **-s** / **-x** / **-z** stay the same.

Singular	Plural	
le bras	les bras	*arms*
la voix	les voix	*voices*
le nez	les nez	*noses*

Words ending in **-al** change to **-aux**.

Singular	Plural	
un animal	des animaux	*animals*
un cheval	des chevaux	*horses*

Words ending in **-eau** / **-eu** add an **x** instead of **s**.

Singular	Plural	
un cadeau	des cadeaux	*presents*
un jeu	des jeux	*games*

Articles

There are two types of articles: definite and indefinite.

In English, the definite article is *the*, and the indefinite articles are *a*, *an* and *some*. In French, both the definite and the indefinite article depend on the gender and number of the noun.

Definite articles

masculine singular	le	le collège	*the school*
masculine plural	les	les collèges	*the schools*
feminine singular	la	la maison	*the house*
feminine plural	les	les maisons	*the houses*

! Unlike in English, the definite article is used in French when you are generalising. **La musique est essentielle.** *Music is essential.*

Indefinite articles

masculine singular	un	un collège	*a school*
masculine plural	des	des collèges	*(some) schools*
feminine singular	une	une maison	*a house*
feminine plural	des	des maisons	*(some) houses*

! The indefinite article is omitted in French when talking about an occupation/profession.
Ma mère est dentiste. *My mother is a dentist.*

However, compare the French and the English in the following sentences.
J'ai des examens aujourd'hui. *I have exams today.*
Elle a des cousins au Sénégal. *She has cousins in Senegal.*

Articles continued

Contractions

Some of the definite articles change when they are combined with **à**.

à + le = <u>au</u>	Elle va <u>au</u> collège.	*She is going to school.*
à + la = <u>à la</u>	Tu vas <u>à la</u> piscine.	*You are going to the swimming pool.*
à + l' = <u>à l'</u>	Elle est <u>à l'</u>hôpital.	*She is at the hospital.*
à + les = <u>aux</u>	J'ai une tarte <u>aux</u> pommes.	*I have an apple tart.*

Similarly, some of the definite articles change when they are combined with **de**.

de + le = <u>du</u>	près <u>du</u> collège	*near the school*
du + la = <u>de la</u>	à côté <u>de la</u> maison	*next to the house*
de + l' = <u>de l'</u>	en face <u>de l'</u>hôtel	*opposite the hotel*
de + les = <u>des</u>	à droite <u>des</u> toilettes	*on the right of the toilet*

Grammar

ADJECTIVES

Adjectives

French adjectives (words that describe nouns) have different endings depending on the noun they describe. The masculine singular form is what you find in a dictionary. Generally, add **-e** for feminine and **-s** for plural.

masculine singular	masculine plural	feminine singular	feminine plural
un pull bleu	des pulls bleus	une veste bleue	des vestes bleues
a blue sweater	(some) blue sweaters	a blue jacket	(some) blue jackets

If a masculine adjective already ends in **-e**, you don't need to add another one for the feminine.

masculine singular	feminine singular
un garçon timide	une fille timide
a shy boy	a shy girl

If a masculine adjective already ends in **-s**, you don't need to add another one for the plural.

masculine singular	masculine plural
un gros gâteau	deux gros gâteaux
a big cake	two big cakes

In the same way, if a masculine adjective ends in **-x**, the plural doesn't change.

masculine singular	masculine plural
un projet ambitieux	des projets ambitieux
an ambitious project	(some) ambitious projects

Here are some common exceptions regarding the feminine form of some adjectives. Some adjectives need a double consonant before the **e** in the feminine.

masculine singular	feminine singular
bon	bonne
gros	grosse
réel	réelle

-eux becomes **-euse** in the feminine.

masculine singular	feminine singular
délicieux	délicieuse
heureux	heureuse

-eau becomes **-elle** in the feminine.

masculine singular	feminine singular
beau	belle
nouveau	nouvelle

Adjectives of nationality

Adjectives of nationality do not begin with a capital letter. Like other adjectives, they take an **-e** at the end in the feminine and an **-s** in the plural – unless there is one there already.

	masculine singular	masculine plural	feminine singular	feminine plural
Scottish	écossais	écossais	écossaise	écossaises
Welsh	gallois	gallois	galloise	galloises
Swiss	suisse	suisses	suisse	suisses

Demonstrative adjectives

These correspond to the English 'this', 'these', 'that' and 'those'. The French equivalents go before the noun.

	singular (this/that)		plural (these/those)	
masculine	ce	ce matin	ces	ces collèges
masculine followed by a vowel or a silent h	cet	cet après-midi cet hôtel	ces	ces ordinateurs ces hôtels
feminine	cette	cette semaine	ces	ces salles de classe

Indefinite adjectives

Unlike most other adjectives, indefinite adjectives go before the noun. Note that **chaque** is always singular and **plusieurs** is always plural.

autre/autres	other	une autre fois	another time
chaque	each	chaque visite	each visit
même/mêmes	same	la même chose	the same thing
plusieurs	several	plusieurs solutions	several solutions
quelque/quelques	a few/some	quelques jours	a few days
tout/tous	all	tout le temps	all the time
toute/toutes		toutes les ressources	all resources

Interrogative adjectives

Quel (meaning *which/what*) agrees with the noun it goes with.

masculine singular	quel	Quel âge as-tu ?	*How old are you?*
masculine plural	quels	Quels sports aimes-tu ?	*What sports do you like?*
feminine singular	quelle	Quelle heure est-il ?	*What time is it?*
feminine plural	quelles	Quelles matières préfères-tu ?	*Which subjects do you prefer?*

Possessive adjectives

These are adjectives like 'my', 'your' and 'our' that indicate possession or ownership. In French, they go before the noun. The possessive adjective agrees with the noun it goes with, not the person who owns it.

> **!** Remember that in French, you don't distinguish between his, her and its.

my	masculine singular	mon	mon père *my father*
	feminine singular*	ma	ma mère *my mother*
	masculine and feminine plural	mes	mes parents *my parents*
your	masculine singular	ton	ton copain *your (boy)friend*
	feminine singular*	ta	ta copine *your (girl)friend*
	masculine and feminine plural	tes	tes amis *your friends*
his / her / its	masculine singular	son	son grand-père *his / her grandfather*
	feminine singular*	sa	sa grand-mère *his / her grandmother*
	masculine and feminine plural	ses	ses grands-parents *his / her grandparents*
our	masculine singular	notre	notre cousin *our (male) cousin*
	feminine singular	notre	notre cousine *our (female) cousin*
	masculine and feminine plural	nos	nos cousins *our cousins*
your	masculine singular	votre	votre appartement *your flat*
	feminine singular	votre	votre maison *your home*
	masculine and feminine plural	vos	vos voisins *your neighbours*
their	masculine singular	leur	leur chien *their dog*
	feminine singular	leur	leur souris *their mouse*
	masculine and feminine plural	leurs	leurs animaux *their pets*

*Before a feminine word that begins with a vowel or a silent **h**, use **mon/ton/son** instead of **ma/ta/sa**. **mon amie** *my friend*   **ton histoire** *your story*   **son infirmière** *his/her/its nurse*

Comparatives and superlatives

These are adjectival phrases that show you are making a comparison: 'more expensive than', 'cleaner', 'as tall as', 'less difficult', etc. The adjectives in the phrases agree with the noun as normal. You can make comparisons by using **plus** / **moins** / **aussi que** + adjective.

Comparatives

-er than … more … than …	plus … que	**Le bus est plus rapide que le vélo.** *The bus is faster than the bike.* **Les trains sont plus chers que les avions.** *Trains are more expensive than planes.*
less … than …	moins … que	**Le parc est moins propre que ton jardin.** *The park is less clean than your garden.*
as … as …	aussi … que	**La montagne est aussi belle que le lac.** *The mountain is as beautiful as the lake.*

! Note that the adjective that follows **plus/moins/aussi** agrees with the noun it refers to.

Some comparatives are irregular.

bon *good*	meilleur/meilleurs meilleure/meilleures *better*	**Les pêches sont meilleures que les pommes ?** *Are peaches better than apples?*
mauvais *bad*	pire/pires *worse*	**Mes notes sont pires que l'année dernière.** *My grades are worse than last year.*

ⓗ Superlatives

the …-est the most…	le/la/les plus …	**le village le plus propre** *the cleanest village* **les endroits les plus agréables** *the most pleasant places*
the least…	le/la/les moins …	**les villes les moins polluées** *the least polluted cities*

Some comparatives are irregular.

meilleur/meilleurs meilleure/meilleures *better*	le meilleur/les meilleurs la meilleure/les meilleures *the best*	**Lila est la meilleure de la classe !** *Lila is the best in the class!*
pire/pires *worse*	le pire/les pires la pire/les pires *the worst*	**C'est le pire jour de l'année.** *It is the worst day of the year.*

Grammar

ADVERBS

Adverbs

Adverbs are words that describe how the action of a verb is being done, such as 'carefully', 'slowly', 'often', 'fast'. They can also be used with an adjective: 'It was really delicious.'

Many French adverbs are formed by adding **-ment** to the feminine singular form of the adjective.

masculine adjective	feminine adjective	adverb
complet	complète	complètement *completely*
lent	lente	lentement *slowly*
premier	première	premièrement *firstly*

There are some exceptions.

masculine adjective	adverb
absolu	absolument *absolutely*
récent	récemment *recently*
vrai	vraiment *truly / really*

Some common adverbs do not end in **-ment**.

bien	well	Elle parle bien.	She speaks well.
mal	badly	Tu chantes mal.	You sing badly.
vite	quickly	Ils mangent vite.	They eat quickly.

As with adjectives, you can make comparisons using **plus/moins/aussi … que**.
Tu cours <u>plus vite que</u> moi. *You run faster than me.*
Il parle <u>moins lentement que</u> le prof. *He speaks less slowly than the teacher.*
Elle travaille <u>aussi bien que</u> son frère. *She works as well as her brother.*

The comparative of **bien** is irregular.

adverb	comparative		
bien	mieux	Tu nages <u>mieux que</u> moi.	*You swim better than me.*

Adverbs of time

après-demain	the day after tomorrow
aujourd'hui	today
avant-hier	the day before yesterday
déjà	already
demain	tomorrow
encore	still / again
hier	yesterday

Adverbs of place

dedans	inside
dehors	outside
ici	here
la	there
là-bas	over there
loin	far
près	nearby
partout	everywhere

Adverbs of frequency

parfois	sometimes
rarement	rarely
souvent	often
toujours	always

Adverbs of sequence

après	after
avant	before

Quantifiers and intensifiers

assez	enough / quite
beaucoup	a lot
peu	little
très	very
trop	too / too much
un peu	a little

Grammar

PRONOUNS

Subject pronouns

Subject pronouns are the words that refer to the person or thing doing the action of the verb. In English, they are found before the verb. For example: 'He is making the dinner.' 'We are watching a film.' 'It is not working.'

je / j'	I	Je suis britannique. / J'aime la musique.	I am British. / I like music.
tu	you (singular, informal)	Tu as quinze ans ?	Are you fifteen?
il	he / it	Il habite au Canada.	He lives in Canada.
elle	she / it	Elle habite en Tunisie.	She lives in Tunisia.
on	we (informal)	On est amis.	We are friends.
nous	we	Nous parlons français.	We speak French.
vous	you (singular, formal) (plural)	Vous comprenez ?	Do you understand?
ils	they (masculine)	Ils regardent une vidéo.	They are watching a video.
elles	they (feminine)	Elles jouent au foot.	They are playing football.

Je is shortened to **j'** in front of a vowel or a silent **h**.
J'habite dans un petit village. *I live in a small village.*

There are two words for you in French: **tu** and **vous**.
- Use **tu** when speaking to one person of your own age or in your family.
- Use **vous** when speaking to an adult not in your family or when speaking to more than one person.

Direct object pronouns – the plural forms are Ⓗ only

A direct object pronoun replaces a noun that is the direct object of the verb (i.e. what or who is receiving the action of the verb).

These pronouns come in front of the verb, unlike in English.
Je le prends. *I am taking it.*   **Elle me comprend.** *She understands me.*

singular	plural
me/m'	nous
te/t'	vous
le/l'	les
la/l'	

Me/te/le/la are shortened to **m'/t'/l'** in front of a vowel or a silent **h**.

Tu m'entends ? *Can you hear me?*

Indirect object pronouns — the plural forms are Ⓗ only

An indirect object pronoun replaces a noun that is the indirect object of the verb. In French, this indirect object is introduced by **à** and comes after the verb. However, the indirect object pronoun comes before the verb, without **à**.

Elle donne un cadeau <u>à son copain</u>. *She gives a present <u>to her boyfriend</u>.*
Elle <u>lui</u> donne un cadeau. *She gives <u>him</u> a present.*

singular	plural
me / m'	nous
te / t'	vous
lui	leur

Relative pronouns: qui, que

Qui and **que** are pronouns that are used to combine two sentences into one.

Qui

Qui is used as the subject of the verb that follows. It can refer to people and things and can be translated as *who, which* or *that*.

Instead of saying:
J'ai une cousine. Elle habite au bord de la mer. *I have a cousin. She lives at the seaside.*
You can say:
J'ai une cousine <u>qui</u> habite au bord de la mer. *I have a cousin <u>who</u> lives at the seaside.*

Another example:
On a acheté l'ordinateur. Il est sur la table. *We bought the computer. It is on the table.* OR
On a acheté l'ordinateur <u>qui</u> est sur la table. *We bought the computer <u>that</u> is on the table.*

Que

Que (**qu'** before a vowel or a silent **h**) is used as object of the verb that follows. It can refer to people and things and can be translated as *who, whom, which* or *that*.

Instead of saying:
Tu détestes le chanteur. Je l'aime. *You hate the singer. I like him.*
You can say:
Tu détestes le chanteur <u>que</u> j'aime. *You hate the singer (<u>whom</u>) I like.*

Instead of saying:
J'adore le livre. Elle le lit. *I love the book. She is reading it.*
You can say:
J'adore le livre <u>qu'</u>elle lit. *I love the book (<u>that</u>) she is reading.*

Although you can leave out its English equivalent, **que** is not optional in French.

If hesitating between **qui** and **que**, check whether the verb that follows already has a subject. If so, the word you need is probably **que**.
C'est le film <u>que</u> je préfère. *That is the film I prefer.*
Je is the subject of the verb, and **que**, referring to **le film**, is the object.

Another tip: **qui** usually has a verb directly after it, whereas **que** has a subject (a pronoun or noun) + verb after it.

Another relative pronoun: où – H only

Où (where) can also be used to link two parts of a sentence.
la maison où j'habite *the house where I live*

Possessive pronouns – H only

These words indicate possession or ownership and replace the noun to which they refer. For example: 'This coffee is <u>yours</u>' ('yours' = your coffee). They agree with the noun that they replace.

masculine singular	feminine singular	masculine plural	feminine plural	
le mien	la mienne	les miens	les miennes	mine
le tien	la tienne	les tiens	les tiennes	yours (singular, informal)
le sien	la sienne	les siens	les siennes	his/hers/its
le nôtre	la nôtre	les nôtres	les nôtres	ours
le vôtre	la vôtre	les vôtres	les vôtres	yours (singular formal, plural)
le leur	la leur	les leurs	les leurs	theirs

Tu préfères <u>le mien</u> ou <u>le tien</u> ? *Do you prefer mine or yours?*

Emphatic pronouns

Emphatic pronouns are used after a preposition, such as **avec**, **chez**, **pour**, **à côté de**.

moi	*me*	**Tu viens <u>avec moi</u> ?** *Are you coming with me?*
toi	*you*	**J'ai un billet <u>pour toi</u>.** *I've got a ticket for you.*

Other emphatic pronouns – H only

moi	me	nous	us
toi	you (singular, informal)	vous	you (singular formal, plural)
lui	him	eux	them (masculine)
elle	her	elles	them (feminine)

As well as after prepositions, you can use these pronouns:

– for emphasis, before the regular subject pronoun.
  Moi, je suis française, et toi, tu es britannique. *I am French and you are British.*

– with phrases such as:
  C'est lui ! *That's him!*   Et toi ? *What about you?*   Toi aussi. *You too.*

– with **-même**:
  J'ai fait ça moi-même ! *I did it myself!*

moi-même	myself	nous-mêmes	ourselves
toi-même	yourself	vous-même / vous-mêmes	yourself / yourselves
lui-même	himself	eux-mêmes	themselves
elle-même	herself	elles-mêmes	themselves

Pronouns en and y – H only

En, as a pronoun, is used to replace a noun that has been introduced with **du/de la/de l'/des**.
Tu as acheté du poisson ? – Oui, j'en ai acheté. *Did you buy any fish? Yes, I bought some.*

Y can often be translated as *there*. It can also be used to replace a noun introduced with **à**.
Il va au Maroc ? – Oui, il y va demain.
Is he going to Morocco? – Yes, he's going there tomorrow.
Tu penses à l'examen ? – Oui, j'y pense.
Are you thinking of the exam? – Yes, I am thinking about it.

Grammar

VERBS AND TENSES

French verbs have different forms and endings depending on who or what is doing the action and whether the action takes place in the past, the present or the future. The verb tables on **pages 161–166** show the pattern of common verbs.

The infinitive

The infinitive is the basic form of the verb, as you find it in a dictionary.
In English, the infinitive starts with to... (e.g. to speak, to have, to be).

In French, infinitives fall into three categories:
Those ending in **-er**, like **parler**, *to speak*, **travailler**, *to work*, **écouter**, *to listen*.
Those ending in **-ir**, like **choisir**, *to choose*, **finir**, *to finish*.
Those ending in **-re**, like **attendre**, *to wait*, **entendre**, *to hear*.

When two verbs follow each other in French, the second one is in the infinitive.
Tu sais <u>nager</u> ? *Can you swim?*
Elle veut <u>arrêter</u>. *She wants to stop.*
J'aime <u>faire</u> du vélo. *I like cycling.*
On voudrait <u>aller</u> au cinéma. *We would like to go to the cinema.*

After the following verbs, you need **à** in front of an infinitive.

aider à	Elle m'aide à faire mes devoirs.	*She is helping me to do my homework.*
apprendre à	Il apprend à jouer du piano.	*He is learning to play the piano.*
arriver à	Tu arrives à te relaxer ?	*Do you manage to relax?*
commencer à	Elle commence à comprendre.	*She is starting to understand.*
continuer à	On continue à faire attention.	*We continue to be careful.*
hésiter à	Ils hésitent à monter.	*They hesitate to go up.*
inviter à	Elles nous invitent à entrer.	*They are inviting us to go in.*
réussir à	J'ai réussi à trouver un emploi.	*I succeeded in finding a job.*

After the following verbs, you need **de** in front of an infinitive.

avoir besoin de	J'ai besoin de travailler.	*I need to work.*
avoir peur de	Il a peur de tomber.	*He is afraid of falling.*
avoir le temps de	Tu as le temps de prendre un café ?	*Do you have time to have a coffee?*
décider de	Elle a décidé d'aller à l'étranger.	*She decided to go abroad.*
empêcher de	Tu m'empêches de me concentrer.	*You stop me from concentrating.*
essayer de	On essaie de finir l'exercice.	*We are trying to finish the exercise.*
finir de	Vous avez fini de manger ?	*Have you finished eating?*
oublier de	J'ai oublié d'apporter mon livre.	*I forgot to bring my book.*
promettre de	Je promets de faire attention	*I promise to be careful.*

The present tense

The present tense is used for actions that are taking place now or take place regularly in the present.

Je révise pour l'examen. *I am revising for the exam.*
J'ai chimie le mardi. *I have chemistry on Tuesdays.*

Remember that, unlike English, there is only one French present tense.
Je travaille = *I work* and *I am working*
Elle parle = *She speaks* and *She is speaking*
Ils vont = *They go* and *They are going*

As in English, the present tense can also be used to express the future, in combination with a time marker.
Je travaille demain. *I am working tomorrow.*
On est en vacances la semaine prochaine. *We are on holiday next week.*

The verb endings change depending on who is doing the action and depending on whether they are **-er**, **-ir** or **re** verbs.

Most verbs follow a regular pattern, as shown in the table below.

-er verbs parler *to speak*	-ir verbs finir *to finish*	-re verbs vendre *to sell*
je parle	je finis	je vends
tu parles	tu finis	tu vends
il/elle/on parle	il/elle/on finit	il/elle/on vend
nous parlons	nous finissons	nous vendons
vous parlez	vous finissez	vous vendez
ils/elles parlent	ils/elles finissent	ils/elles vendent

+ Some verbs are irregular and do not follow these patterns.
Go to **pages 162–166** for details of the most common ones.

The present tense with depuis – H only

The present tense is also used with **depuis** (for / since) to talk about something that started in the past and is still happening now.

J'apprends le français depuis cinq ans. *I have been learning French for five years.*
Il habite à Bristol depuis sa naissance. *He has been living in Bristol since birth.*

The perfect tense

The perfect tense is used to talk about what you, or someone else, did in the past.
J'ai préparé le déjeuner. *I prepared lunch. / I have prepared lunch.*

To make the perfect tense of most verbs, use the present tense of **avoir** + the past participle of the verb you want to use.

j'ai parlé	I spoke / I have spoken
tu as parlé	you spoke / you have spoken
il / elle / on a parlé	he / she / it spoke, he / she / it has spoken, we spoke / we have spoken
nous avons parlé	we spoke / we have spoken
vous avez parlé	you spoke / you have spoken
ils / elles ont parlé	they spoke / they have spoken

Some verbs, however, need the present tense of **être**, instead of **avoir**.

je suis allé / allée	nous sommes allés / allées
tu es allé / allée	vous êtes allé / allée / allés / allées
il est allé, elle est allée, on est allé / allés / allées	ils sont allés, elles sont allées

When using **être**:
- the past participle has an **-e** on the end when the subject is feminine.
  Elle est sortie. She went out.
- the past participle has an **-s** on the end when the subject is plural.
  Ils sont tombés. They fell.   *Elles sont arrivées.* They have arrived.

Here are the main verbs that need **être**. Try to learn them as pairs.

aller	to go	venir	to come
arriver	to arrive	partir	to leave
entrer	to go in	sortir	to go out
monter	to go up / to get on	descendre	to go down / to get off
naître	to be born	mourir	to die
tomber	to fall	rester	to stay

All reflexive verbs also need **être**.

je me suis réveillé / réveillée
tu t'es réveillé / réveillée
il / elle / on s'est réveillé(s) / réveillée(s)
nous nous sommes réveillés / réveillées
vous vous êtes réveillé(s) / réveillée(s)
ils / elles se sont réveillés / réveillées

The perfect infinitive – Ⓗ only

This form uses **avoir** / **être** + past participle. It means 'having done' something. You can use it with **après** to talk about what happened next when the same person is doing both actions.

Après <u>avoir mangé</u>, j'ai téléphoné à ma copine. *After eating, I rang my friend.*
Après <u>être sorti</u> de la maison, il a couru à la gare. *After going out of the house, he ran to the station.*
Après nous <u>être réveillés</u>, nous avons pris notre petit-déjeuner. *After waking up, we had breakfast.*

Use **avoir** if the verb takes **avoir** in the perfect tense, and **être** if it takes **être**. Remember that with **être** the past participle will need to take an **e** if the subject is feminine and an **s** if it is plural.

Après <u>être arrivées</u>, elles m'ont téléphoné. *After arriving, they rang me.*

Word order

When making a negative statement in the perfect tense, **ne** comes before **avoir** / **être** and **pas** comes after.

Je <u>n'</u>ai <u>pas</u> compris. *I didn't understand.*
Elle <u>n'</u>est <u>pas</u> entrée. *She didn't go in.*

The imperfect tense

This tense is used:
- to describe what someone or something was like in the past.
  C'était drôle. *It was funny.*
- to say what was happening at a certain time in the past.
  Je dormais quand elle a téléphoné. *I was asleep when she rang.*
- to describe something that used to happen regularly in the past.
  Il mangeait du poisson tous les jours. *He used to eat fish every day.*
- after **si** to make a suggestion.
  Si on allait à Paris? *Shall we go to Paris?*

To make the imperfect tense, take the **nous** form of the present tense, remove **-ons**, then add the endings of the imperfect. **The plural forms are Ⓗ only**

	finir *to finish*	
present	nous finiss<u>ons</u>	
imperfect	je finiss<u>ais</u>	nous finiss<u>ions</u>
	tu finiss<u>ais</u>	vous finiss<u>iez</u>
	il/elle/on finiss<u>ait</u>	ils/elles finiss<u>aient</u>

Past participles

The past participle is used to make the past tense called the perfect tense. It usually comes after have or has in English, for example, have finished, or has eaten.

The past participle of **-er** verbs ends in **-é**.

aller	to go	allé	gone
donner	to give	donné	given
manger	to eat	mangé	eaten

The past participle of regular **-ir** verbs ends in **-i**.

choisir	to choose	choisi	chosen
finir	to finish	fini	finished

The past participle of regular **-re** verbs ends in **-u**.

attendre	to wait	attendu	waited
vendre	to sell	vendu	sold

Many common verbs have an irregular past participle, but there are only four possible endings:

-é

être	to be	été	been

-is

mettre	to put	mis	put
prendre	to take	pris	taken

-t

dire	to say	dit	said
écrire	to write	écrit	written
faire	to do/make	fait	done/made
ouvrir	to open	ouvert	open

-u

avoir	to have	eu	had
boire	to drink	bu	drunk
devoir	to have to	dû	had to
lire	to read	lu	read
pouvoir	to be able to	pu	able to
venir	to come	venu	come
voir	to see	vu	seen
vouloir	to want	voulu	wanted

The immediate future tense

Use the present tense of **aller** followed by another verb infinitive, to say what someone is going to do or what is going to happen.

je vais étudier	nous allons parler
tu vas manger	vous allez sortir
il / elle va jouer	ils / elles vont danser

Je vais regarder un film. *I am going to watch a film.*
Il ne va pas pleuvoir. *It's not going to rain.*

The future tense – Ⓗ only

The future tense expresses what will happen.
Je voyagerai à l'étranger. *I will travel abroad.*
Il ne fera pas froid. *It won't be cold.*

To form the future tense, add the correct ending to the infinitive of the verb.
For **-re** verbs, remove the final **-e** before adding the endings.

-er verbs parler *to speak*	-ir verbs finir *to finish*	-re verbs vendre *to sell*
je parlerai	je finirai	je vendrai
tu parleras	tu finiras	tu vendras
il / elle / on parlera	il / elle / on finira	il / elle / on vendra
nous parlerons	nous finirons	nous vendrons
vous parlerez	vous finirez	vous vendrez
ils / elles parleront	ils / elles finiront	ils / elles vendront

Some verbs have an irregular stem, instead of the infinitive, but the endings are the same as above.

aller	to go	j'irai
avoir	to have	j'aurai
devoir	to have to	je devrai
être	to be	je serai
faire	to do / make	je ferai
pouvoir	to be able to	je pourrai
savoir	to know	je saurai
venir	to come	je viendrai
voir	to see	je verrai
vouloir	to want	je voudrai

AQA GCSE French | Grammar

The conditional – Ⓗ only

The conditional expresses what 'would' happen.
Je <u>voudrais</u> étudier la médecine. *I <u>would like</u> to study medicine.*
Si j'étais toi, j'<u>irais</u> là-bas. *If I were you, I <u>would go</u> there.*

To form the conditional, use the stem of the future and add the endings of the imperfect.

	future	imperfect	conditional	
parler	je parl<u>erai</u> tu parl<u>eras</u> il/elle/on parl<u>era</u> nous parl<u>erons</u> vous parl<u>erez</u> ils/elles parl<u>eront</u>	je parl<u>ais</u> tu parl<u>ais</u> il/elle/on parl<u>ait</u> nous parl<u>ions</u> vous parl<u>iez</u> ils/elles parl<u>aient</u>	je parl<u>erais</u> tu parl<u>erais</u> il/elle/on parl<u>erait</u> nous parl<u>erions</u> vous parl<u>eriez</u> ils/elles parl<u>eraient</u>	*I would speak*
aller	j'<u>ir</u>ai	j'all<u>ais</u>	j'<u>ir</u>ais	*I would go*
avoir	j'<u>aur</u>ai	j'av<u>ais</u>	j'<u>aur</u>ais	*I would have*
être	je <u>ser</u>ai	j'ét<u>ais</u>	je <u>ser</u>ais	*I would be*
faire	je <u>fer</u>ai	je fais<u>ais</u>	je <u>fer</u>ais	*I would do*

The imperative

Use the imperative to give advice or instructions.
Fais attention. *Be careful.*
Tournez à droite. *Turn right.*

To form the imperative, use the same as the **tu** and **vous** form of the present tense, but remove the pronouns **tu** and **vous**.

With **-er** verbs, also remove the final **-s** from the **tu** form.

	present		imperative	
parler	tu parl<u>es</u>	vous parlez	parl<u>e</u>	parlez
finir	tu finis	vous finissez	finis	finissez
vendre	tu vends	vous vendez	vends	vendez
aller	tu v<u>as</u>	vous allez	va	allez
faire	tu fais	vous faites	fais	faites

Avoir and **être** are irregular. Ⓗ only

	present		imperative	
avoir	tu as	vous avez	<u>aies</u>	<u>ay</u>ez
être	tu es	vous êtes	<u>sois</u>	<u>soy</u>ez

The present participle – H only

The French present participle ends in **-ant**. It is the equivalent of the *-ing* form in English.

To form it, take the **nous** form of the present tense, remove the **-ons** and replace it with **-ant**.

infinitive	present tense	present participle
écouter	nous écoutons	écoutant *listening*
faire	nous faisons	faisant *doing / making*
parler	nous parlons	parlant *speaking*

There are a few exceptions:

infinitive	present participle
avoir	ayant *having*
être	étant *being*
savoir	sachant *knowing*

En + present participle can be used to express the fact that two actions happen at the same time.
Je fais mes devoirs en écoutant de la musique. *I do my homework while listening to music.*
Il gagne de l'argent en travaillant le weekend. *He earns money by working at the weekend.*

Reflexive verbs

Reflexive verbs have an extra pronoun in front of the verb. In the infinitive, they always start with **se** or **s'** in front of the vowel or a silent **h**. The other pronouns are shown in the table below.

present tense	
se réveiller	s'amuser
je me réveille	je m'amuse
tu te réveilles	tu t'amuses
il / elle / on se réveille	il / elle / on s'amuse
nous nous réveillons	nous nous amusons
vous vous réveillez	vous vous amusez
ils / elles se réveillent	ils / elles s'amusent

They are conjugated like other verbs, but – remember – the perfect tense is formed with **être**.

perfect tense	
se réveiller	s'amuser
je me suis réveillé / réveillée	je me suis amusé / amusée
tu t'es réveillé / réveillée	tu t'es amusé / amusée
il / elle / on s'est réveillé(s) / réveillée(s)	il / elle / on s'est amusé(s) / amusée(s)
nous nous sommes réveillés / réveillées	nous nous sommes amusés / amusées
vous vous êtes réveillé(s) / réveillée(s)	vous vous êtes amusé(s) / amusée(s)
ils / elles se sont réveillés / réveillées	ils / elles se sont amusés / amusées

AQA GCSE French | Grammar

Reflexive verbs continued

Ⓗ only

Several other verbs can be used like reflexive verbs to express reciprocity (the equivalent of 'each other).

Nous nous aimons. *We love each other.*
Vous allez vous voir ? *Are you going to see each other?*
Ils se sont rencontrés dans un club. *They met each other in a club.*

Modal verbs

Modal verbs are used to express concepts like ability, permission, necessity and skill.
In French, they are always followed by an infinitive.

Je <u>dois</u> manger. *I have to eat.*
Tu <u>peux</u> choisir. *You can choose.*
Elle <u>veut</u> travailler. *She wants to work.*
Il <u>sait</u> parler espagnol. *He can (knows how to) speak Spanish.*

The passive – Ⓗ only

The passive is used to say what is done to someone or something.
It is formed with **être** followed by a past participle.

active voice	Elle <u>mange</u> le sandwich.	*She is eating the sandwich.*
passive voice	Le sandwich <u>est mangé</u>.	*The sandwich is being eaten.*

You can use **par** (the equivalent of *by*) to indicate who is doing the action.
Le repas est préparé <u>par</u> toute la famille. *The table is prepared <u>by</u> the whole family.*

The passive is used less often than in English as most sentences can be turned round.
<u>On parle</u> français ici. *French <u>is spoken</u> here.*
Le fromage <u>se mange</u> avec du pain. *Cheese <u>is eaten</u> with bread.*

Impersonal verbs

Impersonal verbs are only used with **il**, in all possible tenses.
Il pleut aujourd'hui. Il pleuvait hier. Il va pleuvoir demain.
It's raining today. It was raining yesterday. It is going to rain tomorrow.

Il **neige** follows the same pattern.
Il neige aujourd'hui. Il neigeait hier. Il va neiger demain.
It's snowing today. It was snowing yesterday. It is going to snow tomorrow.

Il y a means both *there is* and *there are*.
Il y a un cinéma. *There is a cinema.*
Il y a beaucoup de restaurants. *There are many restaurants.*

Il faut and **il vaut mieux** are usually followed by an infinitive.
Il faut dormir huit heures par nuit. *You must sleep eight hours a night.*
Il vaut mieux se coucher tôt. *You'd better go to bed early.*

Il est + adjective + **de** + infinitive
Il est interdit d'allumer son téléphone. *It is forbidden to switch on one's phone.*
Il est facile de prendre le bus. *It is easy to take the bus.*

Expressions with avoir

Although **avoir** usually means 'to have', remember to use it in the following contexts.

<u>avoir</u> ... ans	<u>to be</u> ... years old
<u>avoir</u> chaud	<u>to be</u> warm
<u>avoir</u> froid	<u>to be</u> cold
<u>avoir</u> faim	<u>to be</u> hungry
<u>avoir</u> soif	<u>to be</u> thirsty
<u>avoir</u> peur	<u>to be</u> afraid
<u>avoir</u> de la chance	<u>to be</u> lucky

Grammar

PREPOSITIONS

Using prepositions

Prepositions are used to link a noun, a pronoun or an infinitive to another element in the sentence.

Here are the most common ones:

à	at / in / to
après	after
avant	before
avec	with
contre	against
dans	in
de	of / from
depuis	for / since
entre	between
pour	for / in order to
sans	without
sous	under
sur	on
vers	towards

Je révise <u>avec</u> mon copain. *I am revising with my friend.*
Le chat dort <u>sur</u> mon lit. *The cat is asleep on my bed.*
Il a traversé la rue <u>sans</u> regarder. *He crossed the road without looking.*

+ **à and de with definite articles:** See **page 137** on using **à** and **de** with definite articles.

+ **verbs followed by à and de:** Go to **page 148** for advice on using **à** and **de** with verbs.

+ **avant de ⓗ:** When you use **avant** with an infinitive, to say 'before doing something', remember to add **de** before the verb.
J'ai pris mon petit-déjeuner avant de sortir. *I had breakfast before going out.*

+ **après with verbs ⓗ:** Go to **page 151** for advice on using the perfect infinitive.

Grammar

QUESTIONS

Ways of asking

There are three ways of asking a yes/no question:

- You can turn a statement into a question by adding a question mark and making your voice go up at the end.
  Tu veux aller au cinéma ? *Do you want to go to the cinema?*
- You can also add **est-ce que ...** at the start of the statement.
  Est-ce que tu veux aller au cinéma ?
- In more formal contexts, you can change the word order and start with the verb.
  Veux-tu aller au cinéma ?

To ask other questions, you'll need one of these question words:

combien (de) *how much / how many*	Tu as <u>combien de</u> sœurs ?	*How many sisters do you have?*
comment *how*	<u>Comment</u> voyages-tu ?	*How are you travelling?*
où *where*	<u>Où</u> vas-tu ?	*Where are you going?*
pourquoi *why*	<u>Pourquoi</u> elle rit ?	*Why is she laughing?*
quand *when*	Ils arrivent <u>quand</u> ?	*When are they arriving?*
qu'est-ce que *what*	<u>Qu'est-ce qu'</u>il veut ?	*What does he want?*
que *what*	<u>Que</u> regardes-tu ?	*What are you looking at?*
quel / quelle / quels / quelles *what / which*	<u>Quel</u> temps fait-il ?	*What is the weather like?*
	<u>Quelle</u> heure est-il ?	*What time is it?*
qui *who*	C'est <u>qui</u> ?	*Who is it?*
quoi *what*	Tu fais <u>quoi</u> ?	*What are you doing?*

If the question includes a preposition, it goes before the question word.
C'est pour qui ? *Who is it for?*
Tu joues avec quoi ? *What are you playing with?*

AQA GCSE French | Grammar

Grammar

NEGATION

ne ... pas

To make a sentence negative, put **ne** before the verb and **pas** after it.
Je <u>ne</u> vais <u>pas</u> au stade. *I am not going to the stadium.*

Shorten **ne** to **n'** in front of a vowel or a silent **h**.
Ce <u>n'</u>est <u>pas</u> vrai. *That's not true.*

Pay attention to word order with a sentence that uses the perfect tense: **ne** and **pas** go around the part of **avoir** or **être**.
Il <u>n'</u>a <u>pas</u> téléphoné. *He didn't ring.*
Elle <u>n'</u>est <u>jamais</u> partie. *She never left.*

In negative sentences, use **de / d'** instead of **un / une / du / de l' / de la / des**:

J'ai <u>un</u> frère.	Je n'ai pas <u>de</u> frère.	*I don't have a brother.*
Il y a <u>de l'</u>eau.	Il n'y a pas <u>d'</u>eau.	*There is no water.*
Elle voit <u>des</u> animaux.	Elle ne voit pas <u>d'</u>animaux.	*She doesn't see any animals.*

Other common negative phrases:

ne ... jamais	never	Il <u>ne</u> pleut <u>jamais</u>.	*It never rains.*
ne ... personne	nobody	Il <u>n'</u>aide <u>personne</u>.	*He doesn't help anybody.*
personne ne ...		<u>Personne ne</u> m'aide.	*Nobody helps me.*
ne ... rien	nothing	On <u>ne</u> fait <u>rien</u>.	*We don't do anything.*
rien ... ne		<u>Rien ne</u> les intéresse.	*Nothing interests them.*

Some more negative phrases— Ⓗ only

ne ... pas encore	not yet	Je <u>n'</u>ai <u>pas encore</u> vu le film.	*I haven't seen the film yet.*
ne ... plus	not any more	Il <u>ne</u> fume <u>plus</u>.	*He doesn't smoke any more.*
ne ... ni ... ni ...	neither ... nor	Ce <u>n'</u>est <u>ni</u> bon <u>ni</u> mauvais.	*It's neither good nor bad*

> **!** Remember!
> **ne ... que** doesn't make a sentence negative, it just means *only*.
> Je <u>n'</u>ai <u>qu'</u>une sœur. *I only have one sister.*

Grammar

VERB TABLES

Note: In these tables, when a verb forms the perfect tense with **être**, the past participle is shown with two options: masculine and feminine. The plural **-s** is shown added to the ones that are always plural, and in brackets for those that can be either singular or plural.

je suis parti/-ie = **je suis parti** (said by a male person), **je suis partie** (said by a female person)

vous êtes parti(s)/-ie(s) = **vous êtes parti** (speaking to a single male person), **vous êtes partie** (to a single female), **vous êtes partis** (to more than one male or a mixed group), **vous êtes parties** (to two or more females).

Regular -er verbs

Infinitive	Present	Perfect	Imperfect	Future
parler *to speak*	je parle *(I speak)* tu parles il/elle/on parle nous parlons vous parlez ils/elles parlent	j'ai parlé *(I spoke / I have spoken)* tu as parlé il/elle/on a parlé nous avons parlé vous avez parlé ils/elles ont parlé	je parlais *(I was speaking)* tu parlais il/elle/on parlait nous parlions vous parliez ils/elles parlaient	je parlerai *(I will speak)* tu parleras il/elle/on parlera nous parlerons vous parlerez ils/elles parleront

Regular -re verbs

Infinitive	Present	Perfect	Imperfect	Future
vendre *to sell*	je vends tu vends il/elle/on vend nous vendons vous vendez ils/elles vendent	j'ai vendu tu as vendu il/elle/on a vendu nous avons vendu vous avez vendu ils/elles ont vendu	je vendais tu vendais il/elle/on vendait nous vendions vous vendiez ils/elles vendaient	je vendrai tu vendras il/elle/on vendra nous vendrons vous vendrez ils/elles vendront

Regular -ir verbs

Infinitive	Present	Perfect	Imperfect	Future
finir *to finish*	je finis tu finis il/elle/on finit nous finissons vous finissez ils/elles finissent	j'ai fini tu as fini il/elle/on a fini nous avons fini vous avez fini ils/elles ont fini	je finissais tu finissais il/elle/on finissait nous finissions vous finissiez ils/elles finissaient	je finirai tu finiras il/elle/on finira nous finirons vous finirez ils/elles finiront

Regular reflexive verbs — se réveiller *to wake up*

Present	Perfect	Imperfect	Future
je me réveille	je me suis réveillé/-ée	je me réveillais	je me réveillerai
tu te réveilles	tu t'es réveillé/-ée	tu te réveillais	tu te réveilleras
il/elle/on se réveille	il/elle/on s'est réveillé(s)/-ée(s)	il/elle/on se réveillait	il/elle/on se réveillera
nous nous réveillons	nous nous sommes réveillés/-ées	nous nous réveillions	nous nous réveillerons
vous vous réveillez	vous vous êtes réveillé(s)/-ée(s)	vous vous réveilliez	vous vous réveillerez
ils/elles se réveillent	ils/elles se sont réveillés/-ées	ils/elles se réveillent	ils/elles se réveilleront

Irregular verbs

Infinitive	Present	Perfect	Imperfect	Future
aller *to go*	je vais tu vas il/elle/on va nous allons vous allez ils/elles vont	je suis allé/-ée tu es allé/-ée il/elle/on est allé(s)/-ée(s) nous sommes allés/-ées vous êtes allé(s)/-ée(s) ils/elles sont allés/-ées	j'allais tu allais il/elle/on allait nous allions vous alliez ils/elles allaient	j'irai tu iras il/elle/on ira nous irons vous irez ils/elles iront
avoir *to have*	j'ai tu as il/elle/on a nous avons vous avez ils/elles ont	j'ai eu tu as eu il/elle/on a eu nous avons eu vous avez eu ils/elles ont eu	j'avais tu avais il/elle/on avait nous avions vous aviez ils/elles avaient	j'aurai tu auras il/elle/on aura nous aurons vous aurez ils/elles auront
boire *to drink*	je bois tu bois il/elle/on boit nous buvons vous buvez ils/elles boivent	j'ai bu tu as bu il/elle/on a bu nous avons bu vous avez bu ils/elles ont bu	je buvais tu buvais il/elle/on buvait nous buvions vous buviez ils/elles buvaient	je boirai tu boiras il/elle/on boira nous boirons vous boirez ils/elles boiront
connaître *to know*	je connais tu connais il/elle/on connaît nous connaissons vous connaissez ils/elles connaissent	j'ai connu tu as connu il/elle/on a connu nous avons connu vous avez connu ils/elles ont connu	je connaissais tu connaissais il/elle/on connaissait nous connaissions vous connaissiez ils/elles connaissaient	je connaîtrai tu connaîtras il/elle/on connaîtra nous connaîtrons vous connaîtrez ils/elles connaîtront

Irregular verbs continued

Infinitive	Present	Perfect	Imperfect	Future
courir *to run*	je cours tu cours il/elle/on court nous courons vous courez ils/elles courent	j'ai couru tu as couru il/elle/on a couru nous avons couru vous avez couru ils/elles ont couru	je courais tu courais il/elle/on courait nous courions vous couriez ils/elles couraient	je courrai tu courras il/elle/on courra nous courrons vous courrez ils/elles courront
croire *to believe*	je crois tu crois il/elle/on croit nous croyons vous croyez ils/elles croient	j'ai cru tu as cru il/elle/on a cru nous avons cru vous avez cru ils/elles ont cru	je croyais tu croyais il/elle/on croyait nous croyions vous croyiez ils/elles croyaient	je courrai tu courras il/elle/on courra nous courrons vous courrez ils/elles courront
dire *to say*	je dis tu dis il/elle/on dit nous disons vous dites ils/elles disent	j'ai dit tu as dit il/elle/on a dit nous avons dit vous avez dit ils/elles ont dit	je disais tu disais il/elle/on disait nous disions vous disiez ils/elles disaient	je dirai tu diras il/elle/on dira nous dirons vous direz ils/elles diront
devoir *to have to*	je dois tu dois il/elle/on doit nous devons vous devez ils/elles doivent	j'ai dû tu as dû il/elle/on a dû nous avons dû vous avez dû ils/elles ont dû	je devais tu devais il/elle/on devait nous devions vous deviez ils/elles devaient	je devrai tu devras il/elle/on devra nous devrons vous devrez ils/elles devront
dormir *to sleep*	je dors tu dors il/elle/on dort nous dormons vous dormez ils/elles dorment	j'ai dormi tu as dormi il/elle/on a dormi nous avons dormi vous avez dormi ils/elles ont dormi	je dormais tu dormais il/elle/on dormait nous dormions vous dormiez ils/elles dormaient	je dormirai tu dormiras il/elle/on dormira nous dormirons vous dormirez ils/elles dormiront
écrire *to write*	j'écris tu écris il/elle/on écrit nous écrivons vous écrivez ils/elles écrivent	j'ai écrit tu as écrit il/elle/on a écrit nous avons écrit vous avez écrit ils/elles ont écrit	j'écrivais tu écrivais il/elle/on écrivait nous écrivions vous écriviez ils/elles écrivaient	j'écrirai tu écriras il/elle/on écrira nous écrirons vous écrirez ils/elles écriront

Irregular verbs continued

Infinitive	Present	Perfect	Imperfect	Future
être *to be*	je suis tu es il/elle/on est nous sommes vous êtes ils/elles sont	j'ai été tu as été il/elle/on a été nous avons été vous avez été ils/elles ont été	j'étais tu étais il/elle/on était nous étions vous étiez ils/elles étaient	je serai tu seras il/elle/on sera nous serons vous serez ils/elles seront
faire *to do/ make*	je fais tu fais il/elle/on fait nous faisons vous faites ils/elles font	j'ai fait tu as fait il/elle/on a fait nous avons fait vous avez fait ils/elles ont fait	je faisais tu faisais il/elle/on faisait nous faisions vous faisiez ils/elles faisaient	je ferai tu feras il/elle/on fera nous ferons vous ferez ils/elles feront
lire *to read*	je lis tu lis il/elle/on lit nous lisons vous lisez ils/elles lisent	j'ai lu tu as lu il/elle/on a lu nous avons lu vous avez lu ils/elles ont lu	je lisais tu lisais il/elle/on lisait nous lisions vous lisiez ils/elles lisaient	je lirai tu liras il/elle/on lira nous lirons vous lirez ils/elles liront
mettre *to put*	je mets tu mets il/elle/on met nous mettons vous mettez ils/elles mettent	j'ai mis tu as mis il/elle/on a mis nous avons mis vous avez mis ils/elles ont mis	je mettais tu mettais il/elle/on mettait nous mettions vous mettiez ils/elles mettaient	je mettrai tu mettras il/elle/on mettra nous mettrons vous mettrez ils/elles mettront
partir *to go away*	je pars tu pars il/elle/on part nous partons vous partez ils/elles partent	je suis parti/-ie tu es parti/-ie il/elle/on est parti(s)/-ie(s) nous sommes partis/-ies vous êtes parti(s)/-ie(s) ils/elles sont partis/-ies	je partais tu partais il/elle/on partait nous partions vous partiez ils/elles partaient	je partirai tu partiras il/elle/on partira nous partirons vous partirez ils/elles partiront
prendre *to take*	je prends tu prends il/elle/on prend nous prenons vous prenez ils/elles prennent	j'ai pris tu as pris il/elle/on a pris nous avons pris vous avez pris ils/elles ont pris	je prenais tu prenais il/elle/on prenait nous prenions vous preniez ils/elles prenaient	je prendrai tu prendras il/elle/on prendra nous prendrons vous prendrez ils/elles prendront

Infinitive	Present	Perfect	Imperfect	Future
pouvoir *to be able to*	je peux tu peux il/elle/on peut nous pouvons vous pouvez ils/elles peuvent	j'ai pu tu as pu il/elle/on a pu nous avons pu vous avez pu ils/elles ont pu	je pouvais tu pouvais il/elle/on pouvait nous pouvions vous pouviez ils/elles pouvaient	je pourrai tu pourras il/elle/on pourra nous pourrons vous pourrez ils/elles pourront
recevoir *to receive*	je reçois tu reçois il/elle/on reçoit nous recevons vous recevez ils/elles reçoivent	j'ai reçu tu as reçu il/elle/on a reçu nous avons reçu vous avez reçu ils/elles ont reçu	je recevais tu recevais il/elle/on recevait nous recevions vous receviez ils/elles recevaient	je recevrai tu recevras il/elle/on recevra nous recevrons vous recevrez ils/elles recevront
rire *to laugh*	je ris tu ris il/elle/on rit nous rions vous riez ils/elles rient	j'ai ri tu as ri il/elle/on a ri nous avons ri vous avez ri ils/elles ont ri	je riais tu riais il/elle/on riait nous riions vous riiez ils/elles riaient	je saurai tu sauras il/elle/on saura nous saurons vous saurez ils/elles sauront
savoir *to know*	je sais tu sais il/elle/on sait nous savons vous savez ils/elles savent	j'ai su tu as su il/elle/on a su nous avons su vous avez su ils/elles ont su	je savais tu savais il/elle/on savait nous savions vous saviez ils/elles savaient	je saurai tu sauras il/elle/on saura nous saurons vous saurez ils/elles sauront
sortir *to go out*	je sors tu sors il/elle/on sort nous sortons vous sortez ils/elles sortent	je suis sorti/-ie tu es sorti/-ie il/elle/on est sorti(s)/-ie(s) nous sommes sortis/-ies vous êtes sorti(s)/-ie(s) ils/elles sont sortis/-ies	je sortais tu sortais il/elle/on sortait nous sortions vous sortiez ils/elles sortaient	je sortirai tu sortiras il/elle/on sortira nous sortirons vous sortirez ils/elles sortiront
suivre *to follow*	je suis tu suis il/elle/on suit nous suivons vous suivez ils/elles suivent	j'ai suivi tu as suivi il/elle/on a suivi nous avons suivi vous avez suivi ils/elles ont suivi	je suivais tu suivais il/elle/on suivait nous suivions vous suiviez ils/elles suivaient	je suivrai tu suivras il/elle/on suivra nous suivrons vous suivrez ils/elles suivront

Irregular verbs continued

Infinitive	Present	Perfect	Imperfect	Future
venir *to come*	je viens tu viens il/elle/on vient nous venons vous venez ils/elles viennent	je suis venu/-ue tu es venu/-ue il/elle/on est venu(s)/-ue(s) nous sommes venus/-ues vous êtes venu(s)/-ue(s) ils/elles sont venus/-ues	je venais tu venais il/elle/on venait nous venions vous veniez ils/elles venaient	je viendrai tu viendras il/elle/on viendra nous viendrons vous viendrez ils/elles viendront
voir *to see*	je vois je vois il/elle/on voit nous voyons vous voyez ils/elles voient	j'ai vu tu as vu il/elle/on a vu nous avons vu vous avez vu ils/elles ont vu	je voyais tu voyais il/elle/on voyait nous voyions vous voyiez ils/elles voyaient	je verrai tu verras il/elle/on verra nous verrons vous verrez ils/elles verront
vouloir *to want*	je veux tu veux il/elle/on veut nous voulons vous voulez ils/elles veulent	j'ai voulu tu as voulu il/elle/on a voulu nous avons voulu vous avez voulu ils/elles ont voulu	je voulais tu voulais il/elle/on voulait nous voulions vous vouliez ils/elles voulaient	je voudrai tu voudras il/elle/on voudra nous voudrons vous voudrez ils/elles voudront

EXAMINATION PRACTICE ANSWERS

For detail on how the exam will be marked, you can download the mark schemes from the AQA website and marking guidance from **ClearRevise.com**.

Theme 1 People and lifestyle

Reading

01 C   02 E   03 B   [3 marks]

	Model answer	Accept	Reject	Mark
04	They eat pizza and listen to music.			2
05	They discuss it.	They talk together.		1
06	They sometimes argue but it's never serious.	Their arguments are never serious.		1
07	Her little brother is very funny.	Her younger brother makes her laugh every day.		1
08	Both friends and family are important.	She can't imagine life without friends or family.		1

Listening

01 F   02 E   03 D   04 B   [4 marks]

	Model answer	Accept	Reject	Mark
05	Wednesday			1
06	twelve o'clock/12pm	midday		1
07	history		interesting	1
08	ten o'clock/10am	after break		1

Dictation   [10 marks]

09.1 Ma copine adore le poulet.
09.2 Il ne faut pas arriver en retard.
09.3 Le mardi, j'ai un cours d'espagnol.
09.4 Ma sœur voudrait être végétarienne.
09.5 Je ferai mes devoirs de maths ce soir.

Speaking

Role play
Examples of answers and marks awarded, with recording of model responses.   [10 marks]

	2 marks	1 mark	0 marks
01	Oui, j'aime le sport, parce que c'est amusant.	J'aime le sport.	Le sport amusante.
02	Je mange des repas équilibrés.	Je mange équilibré.	Je boire pas alcool.
03	Je suis allé au lit à dix heures.	Dix heures.	Dix.
04	Ce matin j'ai pris une pomme et du thé.	une pomme et du thé	pomme et thé
05	Et toi, tu dors bien ?	Tu dormir bien?	Bon santé?

Photo card

06 Response to content of photos [5 marks]
    Listen to the recording to hear an example of a student talking about the two photos.

07 Photo card unprepared conversation [20 marks]
    Listen to the recording to hear an example of a student answering the questions.

Writing

01 verts

02 aller

03 au

04 bonne

05 aime [5 marks]

06 Translation into French. [10 marks]

English	Model answer	Accept	Reject
I went	Je suis allé/ Je suis allée		other tenses
to school yesterday.	au collège hier	à l'école hier	
I would like	Je voudrais	J'aimerais	J'aime
to go to university.	aller à l'université.		
In my opinion	À mon avis	Pour moi	
history is never boring.	l'histoire n'est jamais ennuyeuse		
She eats fruit every day,	Elle mange des fruits tous les jours,	un fruit	toujours
but she hates apples.	mais elle déteste les pommes.	elle n'aime pas	
He gets on well	Il s'entend bien		Il entendre bien, Il entend bien
with his sister and his parents.	avec sa sœur et ses parents.		

07 **150-word writing task** [Higher tier, 25 marks]

Example:

Voici mes conseils pour être en bonne santé. D'abord, je recommande de prendre des repas équilibrés et de manger des fruits et légumes tous les jours. Bien sûr, il faut éviter de fumer et de boire trop d'alcool car c'est trop dangereux ! En plus, c'est mieux d'être actif et de faire du sport régulièrement. Chaque personne peut choisir ses activités préférées. Moi, personnellement, je fais du vélo et je joue au basket. Si vous n'aimez pas le sport, vous pouvez choisir une autre activité : promener le chien ou danser, par exemple.

L'année dernière, je ne dormais pas assez. En ce moment, je dors huit heures par nuit et c'est mieux. Je buvais aussi trop de café et je ne buvais pas assez d'eau. Maintenant, j'essaie de faire attention. L'année prochaine, je voudrais changer plus de choses. Je vais peut-être arrêter de manger de la viande. Et vous ?

Theme 2   Popular culture

Reading

	Model answer	Accept	Reject	Mark
01	She could invite eight friends to her house. They used to watch cartoons. They played. They ate the cake.	She invited eight friends round. They watched animations. They ate the gâteau.		4
02	She went to a football match with her friends.			1
03	Their team won.	The atmosphere was fantastic.		1
04	She is trying to think of something different.	She is looking for an original idea.		1

Translation into English

	English	Model answer	Accept	Reject	Mark
05	Ma cousine va se marier	My cousin is getting married	will get/will be getting married		1
	l'été prochain.	next summer.			1
06	Mes parents disent	My parents say	are saying		1
	que je sors trop souvent.	that I go out too often	too much		1
07	Il va regarder cette émission	He is going to watch this programme	He will be watching that programme	wrong tense, this emission	1
	avec son meilleur ami.	with his best friend			1
08	Ils regardent le feu d'artifice	They have been watching the fireworks		present tense	1
	depuis une demi-heure.	for half an hour			1
09	Si j'étais cheffe,	If I were/was a chef			1
	je voudrais ouvrir un restaurant à Paris.	I would like to open a restaurant in Paris.	I would want		1

Listening

01   B
02   C
03   E
04   F   [4 marks]
05   A + B
06   A
07   A   [3 marks]

Dictation   [10 marks]

08.1   Je vais jouer aux cartes avec mon frère.

08.2   Je ne voudrais pas être célèbre.

08.3   Elle va sortir avec ses copains ce weekend.

08.4   Il joue du piano depuis trois ans.

08.5   On reçoit souvent des cadeaux de Noël très inutiles.

Speaking

Reading aloud

01   Check your pronunciation by listening to the recording. [5 marks]

Listen to the recording to hear an example of a student answering the questions. [10 marks]

Photo card

02.1 Listen to the recording to hear an example of a student talking about the two photos. [5 marks]

02.2 Listen to the recording to hear a model response of a student answering the questions. [20 marks]

Writing

01   **50-word writing task** 🄵 [10 marks]

Example:
Mon passe-temps préféré, c'est la danse.
Je déteste le sport car c'est trop fatigant.
À la télé, j'aime beaucoup les documentaires sur les animaux.
Ma célébrité préférée est un danseur de ballet portugais. Il est fantastique !
Je ne voudrais pas être célèbre, parce qu'on n'a pas de vie privée.

02   **90-word writing task** 🄵 🄷 [15 marks]

Example:
J'adore la musique et j'apprends à jouer de la guitare. Alors, je préfère les fêtes où on peut écouter de la musique.
J'aime aussi les fêtes de famille et, l'été dernier, je suis allée au mariage de ma tante. Le soir, après le repas, on a dansé. La musique était géniale et je me suis bien amusée.
Cette année, mes grands-parents et mes cousins vont venir chez nous pour Noël. On va décorer la maison avec un sapin et des illuminations. Je voudrais aussi faire des promenades dans la neige.

03   **150-word writing task** 🄷 [25 marks]

Example:
Quand j'avais huit ans, j'adorais la musique. Je passais beaucoup de temps à écouter un chanteur de rap qui s'appelle Soprano. Je connaissais toutes ses chansons, je regardais toutes ses vidéos et j'essayais de l'imiter. Je voulais chanter comme lui et porter les mêmes vêtements que lui. Mes parents trouvaient ça très drôle.
Si j'étais célèbre, je voudrais être un bon modèle et encourager les gens à faire du sport et à avoir une vie saine. En plus, si j'étais riche un jour, je voudrais aider les gens dans le besoin. Alors, j'essaierais de partager mon argent avec les autres. Je pense aussi qu'il faut s'amuser dans la vie, alors j'espère que je serais une célébrité drôle, avec le sens de l'humour. De toute manière, je ne veux pas être célèbre parce que c'est vraiment trop stressant. Je préfère avoir une vie privée avec ma famille et mes vrais amis.

Theme 3 Communication and the world around us

Reading

01 P + N, 02 P, 03 N, 04 P + N [4 marks]

	Model answer	Accept	Reject	Mark
05	in a house in a village	in a village		1
06	It was far from anywhere. You needed a car to go anywhere.	You needed a car to go to school. You needed a car to go to the supermarket. You needed a car to go and see your friends.		2
07	She lives in a town, in a (small) flat	apartment		2
08	There is a lot of pollution.	It's more polluted than the countryside.		1
09	Two of the following points: – a house in the countryside – no pollution – a large garden to grow fruit and vegetables – in a quiet place, but not completely isolated from the rest of the world			2
10	She needs a bus stop near the house	by bus / on the bus		1

Listening

01 F, 02 D, 03 C, 04 B [4 marks]

05 2N, 06 1F [4 marks]

Dictation [10 marks]

07.1 J'aime jouer en ligne.

07.2 Il va pleuvoir demain.

07.3 Il faut protéger la planète.

07.4 Mon écran d'ordinateur est cassé.

07.5 Je partage mes photos avec mes amis.

Speaking

Role play

Examples of answers and marks awarded: [10 marks]

	2 marks	1 mark	0 marks
01	Je préfère voyager en voiture, parce que c'est plus facile.	Je préfère la voiture.	
02	Je suis allé au bord de la mer. C'était super, parce qu'il faisait beau et il y avait beaucoup de choses à faire.	Je suis allé au bord de la mer.	
03	Quand je suis en vacances, j'utilise une appli pour regarder les cartes.	une appli pour les cartes	J'aime internet
04	Qu'est-ce que tu aimes faire en vacances ?	Toi en vacances ?	Et toi?
05	Je voudrais habiter en centre-ville, dans un quartier animé avec un beau parc.	Je voudrais en ville	

Reading aloud

06 Check your pronunciation by listening to the recording. Then listen to a model response to the questions. [5 + 10 marks]

Photo card

07 Listen to the recording to hear an example of a student talking about the two photos. [5 marks]

08 Listen to the recording to hear a model response of a student answering the questions. [20 marks]

AQA GCSE French – Answers

Writing

	2 marks	1 mark	0 marks
01	Je vois la plage et la mer.	La mer.	Tu vas plage ?
	Il y a aussi des personnes à vélo.	Des vélos aussi.	Je voudrais vélo.
	Il fait beau et chaud.	Il est beau.	Chaud
	C'est les vacances d'été.	Les vacances.	Je prends le bateau.
	Tout le monde se relaxe.	Se relaxer.	Fatigué.

02 Translation into French. [10 marks]

English	Model answer	Accept	Reject
Turn off	Éteins / Éteignez	Éteindre	Tourne/Tournez
the light.	la lumière.		
Yesterday I went	Hier je suis allé/allée		
to town by car.	en ville en voiture.		en car
It is essential	Il est essentiel	C'est essentiel	
to protect the planet.	de protéger la planète.		
I am going to spend my holiday	Je vais passer mes vacances	Je passe/Je passerai	
abroad next year.	à l'étranger l'année prochaine.	dans un pays étranger	
We have started	On a commencé / Nous avons commencé		
to grow vegetables in the garden.	à cultiver des légumes dans le jardin.		

03 **150-word writing task** 🇭 [25 marks]
Example:
En ce moment, j'habite dans un appartement, dans le centre-ville. Nous avons un petit balcon, mais nous n'avons pas de jardin. C'est pratique bien sûr, parce que mon collège est à seulement cinq minutes à pied. Ma rue est très animée avec beaucoup de magasins et de cafés. En plus, le samedi, il y a un marché tout près. C'est vraiment sympa, mais il y a beaucoup trop de bruit. Je voudrais être dans un endroit plus calme.

Dans l'avenir, j'aimerais continuer à vivre en ville, mais je rêve d'un quartier moderne, mieux organisé, où les voitures seraient interdites. Par contre, il y aurait beaucoup de bus électriques très fréquents. Je voudrais aussi beaucoup d'espaces verts pour se relaxer et faire du sport. En plus, tout le monde pourrait avoir un jardin pour cultiver des légumes et des fruits. Ce serait meilleur pour la santé physique et mentale !

GUIDANCE ON GETTING TOP MARKS

> **+ Download pack**
>
> A full online version of this guidance gives you more advice on how to develop your answers progressively through the full range of marks. Download the complete pack from **ClearRevise.com**

Listening exam — Paper 1

F Foundation and **H** Higher tiers | Full marks

In **Section A** of the exam, questions will either be multiple choice or they will need to be answered in English. In **Section B** you will have a dictation task where you need to write down what you hear in French. For the dictation there will be about 20 words in French at Foundation tier and about 30 at Higher. You will hear each item **twice** in Section A and **three** times in Section B.

Section A

In Section A, these are some of the types of question you will hear:

- **Positive/Negative/Positive + Negative.** In this type of question, you will hear what people think about something. You write P if you think it is all positive; N if it is all negative; P+N if you think there is a mixture of both. Listen very carefully. You may hear **intéressant** on the first hearing, but just check what comes just before when you hear it for the second time. **Je trouve ça intéressant** is positive, but **je ne trouve pas ça intéressant** is negative.
- **Choosing A, B or A+B.** You will hear someone speaking and you have to decide whether statement A, statement B or both A+B are correct. You may be sure that one of them is correct on the first hearing, but listen carefully on the second hearing to make sure the other statement isn't also correct.

Section B

In Section B, for the dictation, you will hear a number of short sentences in French. Usually there will be **four** sentences at Foundation tier and **five** at Higher. For each sentence, this is what happens:
- you hear the whole sentence.
- you hear the sentence broken up into two or three sections.
- you hear the whole sentence again.

If you hear it for the first time and there is something you miss, don't panic! You still have two chances to hear it again and get it right.

> **! Remember:** At the end of the exam, you have 2 minutes to check your answers in the whole paper. This gives you a chance to look again at what you have written for the dictation and to spot any careless errors you may have made.

Speaking exam — Paper 2

The exam is divided into **three** sections which are the Role play; the Reading aloud of a text followed by 4 questions; the description of two Photo cards, followed by a conversation on the same theme as the photos. Below are some tips when you are aiming for full marks.

Role play

F Foundation | Full marks

- In order to get the full 10 marks, you will need to complete the five tasks by using a verb in each case. You will usually be asked to give an opinion. **J'aime** (*I like*) is often a possible verb to use. For example, if the task is 'Give your opinion on means of transport in your area', you can say **J'aime le vélo**. If you have forgotten the word **moyen de transport**, name one means of transport you know the French for: **J'aime le vélo**. This will still get two marks.
- For one of the tasks, you will have to ask a question. This can sometimes look trickier than the others. Let's say the task is 'Ask your friend a question about their school'. There are many questions you could ask, but one of them would be to ask 'Do you like your school?' (**Tu aimes ton collège ?**).

H Higher | Full marks

- Look at the advice given for Foundation tier about the task where you have to ask a question. The question-asking task at Foundation and Higher tiers is very similar as regards the level of difficulty.
- The instructions say that you must use at least one verb in each task. Each task is worth 2 marks, whether one or two details are needed. You may also be asked to give one or two advantages or disadvantages in a task. Learn a selection of positive and negative adjectives for this kind of task. Positive ones include: **intéressant** (*interesting*); **amusant** (*good fun*); **passionnant** (*fascinating*); **facile** (*easy*); **utile** (*useful*). Negative ones could be: **ennuyeux** (*boring*); **difficile** (*difficult*); **dangereux** (*dangerous*); **inutile** (*useless*); **cher** (*expensive*). If the task asks for two disadvantages of going to the cinema, you could say **C'est ennuyeux et cher** (even if you think it's fantastic!).

> **!** **Remember:** In the Role play, always try to use language that you are confident you know the French for. The exam is not a time to make things up unless you really have to!

Reading aloud a text

- The main difference between Foundation and Higher tiers is the length of the text. There is a minimum **35 words for Foundation** and **50 words for Higher**. There may be some words at Higher tier that are longer ones, but the pronunciation rules are always the same.
  For example, **-ent** at the end of verbs (in the plural form) is always silent, so **ils parlent** (*they speak / are speaking*) is pronounced like **il parle** (*he speaks / is speaking*).

Reading aloud a text continued

- Practise reading French aloud at home. If you get to a word that you are not sure how to pronounce, you can use a free online dictionary to help. Many of them include a function where by clicking **Écouter** you can listen to the word being pronounced. Some of these also allow you to hear a word pronounced at half speed which can make things easier at first. You can also try typing '*pronounce … in French*' on YouTube or Google. There are several sites that will pronounce the word for you. Try it with a tricky word like **ennuyeux** ('*boring*'). There will usually be more than one example. If one seems very fast, try another. AQA also have a pre-recorded sound bank of the complete vocabulary list available on their website.
- If there is a longer word in the text, break it down into syllables during the preparation time before the exam and write it down on your notes sheet that you can use during the exam. For example, **extraordinaire** ('*extraordinary*'): EX-TRA-OR-DIN-AIRE. You can then look at this when **extraordinaire** appears in the text. Practise separating words out like this at home.
- If there is an accent on an 'e' at the end of a word, it changes the pronunciation. So, to show how the French word **arrivé** is pronounced, it could be noted down as AR-RIV-AY– which is different from **arrive** (no accent) that you could note down as AR-RIV.
- To get the full 5 marks for reading out the text you don't have to be perfect. Concentrate on what you see as the trickiest words and note them down as suggested above. This will help you to make as few errors as possible and you may even be perfect!

> **!** **Remember:** Take your time when reading the text. There are no extra marks for reading it quickly and, if you read it too quickly, you are more likely to mispronounce words.

Reading aloud a text – compulsory questions

After you have read the text, your teacher will ask you four questions. This is the case for both Foundation and Higher tiers, but the questions are slightly harder at Higher.

However, all questions at both tiers will be in the present tense and the mark scheme is the same for both tiers.

F Foundation and **H** Higher | Full marks

- To score full marks, you must answer all questions clearly.
- Two of your answers have to contain at least three verbs. For example:
  – Qu'est-ce que tu fais sur ton portable ?
  – <u>J'envoie</u> des messages à mes amis, <u>j'écoute</u> de la musique et <u>je regarde</u> des vidéos. (verbs underlined).
- One of your other answers must contain two verbs. For example:
  – Que penses-tu de la téléréalité ?
  – <u>Je n'aime pas</u> ça car <u>c'est</u> ennuyeux. (verbs underlined).
- Your other answer can be as little as one word, provided it answers the question clearly. For example:
  – Comment est ton portable ? Noir.

Speaking exam continued

Description of the photos

F Foundation | Full marks

- Try to find 12 things or people in the photos that you definitely know the French for. List them by writing, for example: **Sur la photo 1, je vois une fille, un garçon et un chien**.

H Higher | Full marks

- Add as many other words as you can, to get to around 15 or 16 bits of information in total.
- You can always say what is happening in the photos or what the people are doing, for example: **Il fait beau et les jeunes jouent au foot**.

Conversation

F Foundation | Full marks

- Wherever possible, give an extra piece of information when you answer a question and use a verb when you do. For example, your teacher asks you what you do with your friends: **Qu'est-ce que tu fais avec tes amis ?** You could talk about some of the places where you go: **On va au cinéma ou au parc**. That is a good answer, but you only use one verb (**va**). If you can use more than one verb, do it! For example: **On va au parc et on joue au foot**.
- Vary what you say as much as you can and avoid repeating the same common language such as **j'aime**. You can always use **j'adore** instead or adjectives that say why you might like something: **amusant / fantastique / génial / super**.

H Higher | Full marks

- Try to answer most of the questions by using at least three verbs. There will be some occasions where you feel you can go beyond three. For example, you spend a lot of time on your mobile and your teacher asks you how you use technology: **Comment est-ce que tu utilises la technologie ?** You might think of quite a lot to say, using several verbs: **J'utilise mon portable tous les jours pour communiquer avec mes amis. Hier soir, j'ai appelé ma meilleure amie et nous avons parlé de nos projets de vacances. C'était sympa**. Don't give very long answers too often, though.
- Your French should be mostly accurate and include a wide variety of different language with some more complex structures. Learn things like **quand je serai plus âgé** (*when I'm older*); **je viens de voir ...** (*I've just seen ...*); **j'étudie le français depuis cinq ans** (*I've been studying French for five years*); **on devrait faire plus de choses pour ...** (*we should do more in order to ...*).

Reading exam — Paper 3

In **Section A** of the exam, questions will either be multiple choice or they will need to be answered in **English**. In **Section B** you will translate some sentences from **French into English**. At Foundation tier, there will be about **35** words to translate and at Higher there will be about **50**.

F Foundation and **H** Higher | Full marks

Section A

In Section A, these are some of the types of question you will see:

- **Positive / Negative / Positive + Negative.** In this type of question, you will read what people think about something. You write P if you think it is all positive; N if it is all negative; P+N if you think there is a mixture of both. Read the text carefully. If you see the word **stressant**, just check whether it says, for example, **c'est stressant** (N) or **ce n'est jamais stressant** (P).

- **Choosing A, B or A+B.** You will read a text and you have to decide whether statement A, statement B or both A+B are correct. You may be sure that one of them is correct, but read the rest of the text carefully to make sure the other statement isn't also correct.

Section B

In Section B you have to translate some French sentences into English. Don't leave any gaps. A guess always has a chance of being right; a gap doesn't. When you finish translating a sentence, read what you have written and make sure it makes sense. If it doesn't, there will be a mistake somewhere.

AQA GCSE French

Writing exam   Paper 4

F Foundation | Full marks

Question 1

Find 5 things in the photo that you definitely know the French for and write 5 sentences all beginning with **Il y a** (*there is/there are*), for example: **Il y a une femme**. Each sentence you write is worth 2 marks.

If you can't find 5 things, you can always say what someone is doing, for example: **La femme court**; or you may be able to say what the weather is like if the photo is outside, for example: **Il fait beau**.

Question 2

You must write something that is clearly understandable about all 5 bullet points. You need to write about 50 words in total, which works out at around 10 words per bullet point. However, you can still get full marks if you write more about some of the bullet points than others.

Try to vary your language as much as you can, but it doesn't need to be complicated. For example, let's say one of the bullet points is **La nourriture**. You could write: **J'aime manger des legumes parce que c'est bon pur la santé. Je déteste les frites. Je déteste** (*I hate*) is used instead of **Je n'aime pas** to avoid repeating the verb **aime**.

Question 3

For each question, look carefully at the three words you have to choose from. Verb endings and agreement of adjectives are always very important. For example: **Ma copine est intelligente** – *My* (female) *friend is clever*. The word for 'is', is **est** and the adjective **intelligente** ends in an 'e' because a female person is being described.

Always write the word you have chosen in the space and be sure to spell the word correctly, including accents, or you will not get the mark.

Question 4 (translation)

When it is marked, the translation is divided into 15 sections. Each time you translate a section accurately enough to convey the meaning, you are given a tick. The ticks are added up and you get a mark out of 5 as follows: 13–15 ticks = 5 marks; 10–12 = 4; 7–9 = 3; 4–6 = 2; 1–3 = 1. There are a further 5 marks that are given for grammatical accuracy. The exam paper doesn't show what the 15 sections are.

Have a go at everything. If you leave any blanks because you don't know a word, you will lose marks. The examiner will have to assume that if you had given it a go, you would have got it wrong anyway, so you might as well try something.

As we saw in Question 3, verb endings and adjectives are important, so always check what you have written is absolutely clear. If you make a mistake and have to correct it, cross out the incorrect word and write the other one clearly. Don't write in very small handwriting to get the correct word into a small gap because it may not be clear enough for the examiner.

Question 5

You have two questions to choose from, but you should only answer one of them. Have a good look at the bullet points in each question before you start and think about which is the one where you feel most comfortable that you can write around **90** words in French.

To get full marks, you will have to give clear information about all three bullet points.

Writing exam, Foundation tier continued

This means that you will have to use three time frames to cover the present, past and future bullet points successfully.

You need to write around **90** words in total, which works out at about **30** words per bullet point. You won't be penalised if you write more on one bullet point than the others, but it is a good idea to have roughly the same amount of words for each one. This is because you are asked to develop your ideas regularly. For example, let's say that one bullet point asks you to write about what you do at the weekend. You could just write: **Le weekend je vais au parc**. This is enough to cover the bullet point successfully. However, you would only be saying one thing. If you go on to write about **30** words, you will be developing your ideas, in other words writing more about what you do. Giving opinions is always a good way to develop what you write. This is what you could write: **Le weekend je vais au parc avec mes amis. On joue au foot ou on fait du skate. On s'amuse bien. Quelquefois je vais chez mes grands-parents et on fait des gâteaux ensemble. C'est sympa.**

For Assessment Objective 3 (AO3) you will need a good variety of vocabulary, so try not to repeat words wherever possible. Your writing should be as accurate as you can get it, but it doesn't have to be perfect. Vary your language, maybe by using some of these expressions:

- **cependant** – *however*
- **en plus** – *besides*, *also* (a good alternative to **aussi**)
- **par contre** – *on the other hand*
- **qui** – *who* (a good way to link separate phrases to make one longer sentence – **je vais chez ma copine qui habite en ville**)
- **par exemple** – *for example*

Higher | Full marks

Question 1 (translation)
See the notes for Foundation Question 4. The requirements are the same at both tiers.

Question 2
See the notes for Foundation Question 5. The questions and mark scheme are identical at both tiers.

Question 3
There are 25 marks in total: 15 for Assessment Objective 2 (AO2), which is for writing around 150 words in clearly understandable French and for developing ideas and descriptions; 5 marks for AO3 range and use of language, which is for having a variety of vocabulary and grammatical structures and for being able to produce more complex language; 5 marks for AO3 accuracy, in other words the fewer mistakes you make, the better.

On AQA's website there is a copy of the mark scheme for the Higher, as well as the Foundation, papers. You will find examples of what is meant by development, variety of language and complex language. It is a good idea to look at this so you can see what examiners will be looking for.

You have two questions to choose from, but you should only answer one of them. Have a good look at the bullet points in each question before you start. Decide which one you feel most comfortable writing enough about to use around 150 words in French.

You need to write clear information in relation to both bullet points and develop your ideas and descriptions regularly. Giving opinions and reasons is often a good way to do this.

There must be a very good variety of vocabulary, so try to impress by including as many different words as you can.

You must use complex language regularly. Remember you can see examples on AQA's website.

The two bullet points will refer to different time frames. Usually, one point will need you to answer in the present tense and the other will refer either to the past or to the future. Make sure you have used the correct tenses and endings for the verbs in each bullet point.

INDEX

Verb types
-er verbs 161
-ing verbs 134
-ir verbs 161
-re verbs 161

A
active voice 156
adjectives 10, 12, 138
adverbs 109, 142
advice
  conversation 176
  listening 173
  photo card 176
  reading aloud 174
  role play 174
  translation 179
all 66
aller 24
articles 136
avant de 158
avoir 11, 157

B
bank holidays 65
bedroom 117
body parts 26

C
Christmas 70
climate 124
colours 4
comparatives 141
comparisons 13
conditional 83, 99, 154
conjugation 81
contractions 137
conversation advice 176
could, should and would 82

D
days of the week 2
definite article 136
demonstrative adjectives 139
dictation 23, 39, 57, 69, 81, 88, 102, 105, 125, 130
direct object pronouns 144
Diwali 64

E
emphatic pronouns 146
environment 122
être 11

F
faire 24
family 10
food and drink 20
for and since 67
frequency 143
friends 10, 14
future 58
future tense 57, 153

G
grammar 133
greetings 4

I
immediate future tense 153
imperative 28, 122, 154
imperfect tense 25, 83, 151
impersonal verbs 157
indefinite adjectives 139
indefinite article 136
indirect object pronouns 145
inference questions 42
infinitive form 25, 51, 61, 125, 134, 148
intensifiers 143
internet 106
interrogative adjectives 139
irregular verbs 162

J
jobs 37, 74, 134

L
liaisons 5
likes and dislikes 20

M
modal verbs 96, 156
months 3

N
nationality 11, 139
near future tense 37, 57
negation 160
nouns 134
numbers 3

O
often 22
opinions 4, 51

P
pain 26
passive voice 156
past 58
past participles 152
perfect infinitive 151
perfect tense 25, 150
phones 104
phonics 5
photo card 19, 31, 67, 77, 89, 103, 115, 119, 127
photo card advice 176
place 143
plurals of nouns 135
position 119
possessive adjectives 140
possessive pronouns 146
prepositions 158
present time frame 58
present participle 155
present tense 25, 28, 80, 122, 149
pronouns 144

Q

quantifiers 143
que 145
questions 9, 159
qui 145

R

reading advice 177
reading aloud 35, 37, 55, 65, 74, 89, 92, 108, 118, 123, 131
reading aloud advice 174
reflexive verbs 16, 155, 162
relative pronouns 145, 146
role play 19, 27, 43, 51, 59, 63, 85, 111
role play advice 174

S

school 32, 34
seasons 3
sequence 143
should, could and would 82
simple future tense 57
speaking advice 174
subject pronouns 144
subjects (school) 32
superlatives 141

T

tenses 148
  conditional 83, 99, 154
  future 153
  immediate future 153
  imperative 154
  imperfect 25, 151
  near future 37, 57
  perfect 25, 150
  perfect infinitive form 151
  present 25, 149
  simple future 57
time 2, 143
time frames 58
timetable 33
translation advice 179
transport 92

V

verbs 148
  impersonal 157
  infinitive 25, 148
  irregular 162
  modal 156
  passive 156
  reflexive 16, 155, 162
verb tables 161
vocabulary 44, 86, 128

W

weather 94
would 99
  (could and should) 82
writing advice 178

NOTES, DOODLES AND EXAM DATES

Doodles

Exam dates

Listening:
Reading:
Speaking:
Writing:

EXAMINATION TIPS

When you practise examination questions, use the following tips collated from years of experience and examiner reports to help you maximise your result.

Written exams (Listening, Reading, Writing)

1. Ensure your handwriting is clear and legible.
2. Cross out any mistakes with one clear line.
3. Read the question instructions carefully.
4. **For Listening:**
   - Don't write answers while the recording is playing. Wait for the pause between the two recordings of a question or the pause between one question and the next.
   - In the dictation, you will hear everything three times in total. Check your spellings when you hear each section.
5. **For Reading:**
   - Read forwards and backwards in a text from the key word in the question. Sometimes the answer comes after the key word and sometimes it comes before. Translate every word in the paragraph.
6. **For Listening and Reading:**
   - Look at the heading of the question. It is in English and gives you the question context, for example 'School'.
   - If you are asked to give a certain number of details, only give that number.
   - When answering with a letter, make sure the letter is written clearly. For example, the letter A can look like an H if you leave a gap at the top.
   - Don't leave any answers blank. A blank response will always score 0 but a guess may get a mark.
7. **For Writing:**
   - If a question asks you to write an approximate number of words, try to keep to roughly that number. If you write much more than that, you may make more errors and this can lead to a lower mark.
   - Mention all of the bullet points in an answer and tick them off on the question paper as you cover them.
   - Check that you don't miss out any parts of the translation.
   - Check your work carefully, especially verb tenses and endings.

Speaking exam

8. Use the 15 minutes of preparation time wisely. You can write down exactly what you are going to say for the role play and for the description of the photos. For the reading aloud passage, you can write down tricky words as you will say them, for example *yaourt* as *yow-oort* or *croissant* as *kwas-on*.
9. You can ask for repetition of a question in any part of the test, but make sure you ask in French. You can say **Vous pouvez répéter, s'il vous plaît ?**
10. Speak clearly at all times and don't read your notes from the preparation time too fast. There are no extra marks for speaking quickly.

Bonne chance !

New titles coming soon!

These guides are everything you need to ace your exams and beam with pride. Each topic is laid out in a beautifully illustrated format that is clear, approachable and as concise and simple as possible.

They have been expertly compiled and edited by subject specialists, highly experienced examiners, industry professionals and a good dollop of scientific research into what makes revision most effective. Past examination questions are essential to good preparation, improving understanding and confidence.

- Hundreds of marks worth of examination style questions
- Answers provided for all questions within the books
- Illustrated topics to improve memory and recall
- Specification references for every topic
- Examination tips and techniques
- Free Python solutions pack (CS Only)

Absolute clarity is the aim.

Explore the series and add to your collection at **www.clearrevise.com**

Available from all good book shops

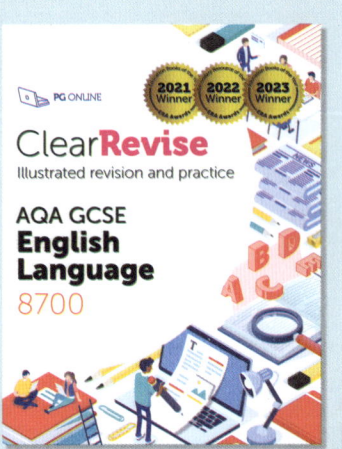

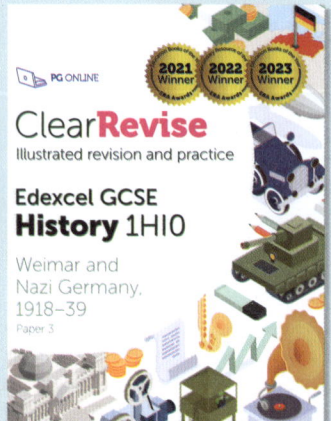

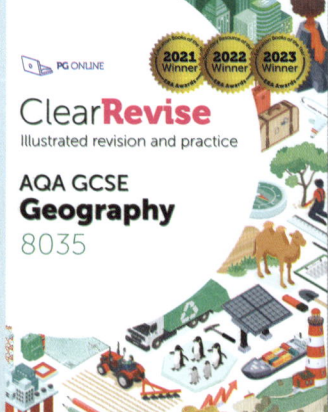

amazon   @pgonlinepub

ClearRevise — Illustrated revision and practice

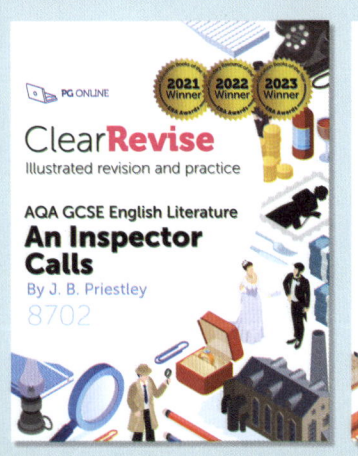

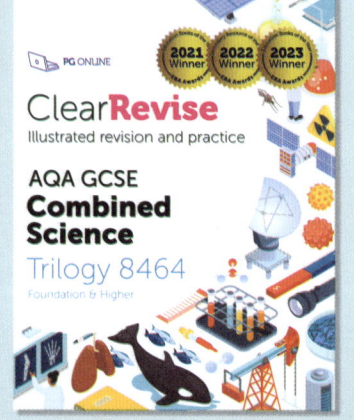

- AQA GCSE **Spanish** 8692 — Foundation & Higher
- AQA GCSE **German** 8662 — Foundation & Higher
- AQA GCSE **English Language** 8700
- Edexcel GCSE **History 1HI0** — Weimar and Nazi Germany, 1918–39, Paper 3
- AQA GCSE **Geography** 8035
- OCR GCSE **Computer Science** J277
- AQA GCSE English Literature **An Inspector Calls** By J. B. Priestley 8702
- Edexcel GCSE **Business** 1BS0
- AQA GCSE **Combined Science** Trilogy 8464 — Foundation & Higher
- AQA GCSE **Design and Technology** 8552